Ideal and Practice in Public Administration

EMMETTE S. REDFORD

Ideal and Practice in Public Administration

University of Alabama Press 1958

PRINTED AND BOUND BY THE BIRMINGHAM PRINTING CO.
BIRMINGHAM, ALA.
LIBRARY OF CONGRESS CATALOG CARD NO. 57-14937

Preface

THE SIX CHAPTERS in this little book were presented as lectures in the annual lecture series in public administration at the University of Alabama.

It was a great pleasure to spend a week at the University of Alabama, where a distinctive and distinguished program of research, teaching, and service in public affairs has been developed, first under the leadership of Roscoe Martin and then of York Willbern, lately assisted by Robert Highsaw. The lectures are themselves a unique development in the educational program. Though given to a wider audience, they are a part of the training program for the Alabama-Tennessee-Kentucky Fellows in Public Administration. The Fellows and the faculty in political science form a lively center of discussion and inquiry during the week of the lectures, which makes the week a memorable one in the experience of the lecturer.

I am grateful to Professors York Willbern, Robert Highsaw, and Donald Strong of the University of Alabama and to my colleague at the University of Texas, Professor Alton Burdine, for reading the lectures. And to my colleague Professor Clarence Ayres for reading Chapter 5. All have offered suggestions which helped me in the revisions before publication.

EMMETTE S. REDFORD

The University of Texas

Contents

By Way of Introduction

IT HAS NO well-defined ideals," said Dean Roscoe Pound of public administration.[1] This is an indictment against administration, for it is a statement of conclusion that administration does not merit the trust the judiciary has earned. The indictment is serious, for administration today has vital functions in national defense, domestic prosperity, and personal security. If it has no ideals which can guide its conduct and against which its trends and results can be evaluated, then hope for its constructive service for the welfare of man must be dim.

Is there a public philosophy for administration? Can the philosophy be stated with reasonable clarity? Is the philosophy consonant with reality, with things as they are or as they may be? Have we built a behemoth in our midst which moves only by the propulsions of circumstance toward no end at all? Or is there virtue, measured by the needs and ideals of man, in the inner workings and outward effects of this new giant?

These are, in my opinion, timely questions. Social study has in our day been tempted into the garden of science. The trend is toward behaviorism, in which study is concentrated on the actions of men and the in-

1 Roscoe Pound, *Administrative Law* (Pittsburgh, 1942), p. 5. Pound used the terms "administration" and "administrative process" interchangeably and broadly in the cited discussion.

terrelations among events rather than upon their ethical significance. The student of society, including that of administration, should eat heartily of this apple. But other fruit must be eaten also if the student is to perceive good and evil and the ways in which social institutions and human behavior may be ordered toward the good. As Stephen K. Bailey has so eloquently told us: in this day when "our social and political world is still 'skirting the rim of hell'," the "real frontier," the "everlasting frontier for administrators, legislators, and scholars," is the "frontier of the good life, the humane goal, the civilized means," and the most important consideration is the "exercise of will and moral choice."[2]

Dean Pound's indictment is a challenge to students of administration, for they have considered administration to be not merely inevitable but potentially an instrument for human service. I have accepted the challenge in choosing the subject of these lectures. In doing so I realize that much will be said which is beyond absolute proof and some things with which persons of good judgment will disagree. This in a measure confirms Dean Pound's charge that the ideals of administration are not "well-defined"; more largely, however, the differences of judgment arise because of the uncertainties as to the ways in which ideals may be realized in practice. But imperfect definition is not always an indication of lack of existence, for ideals may be replete with varieties of meanings; nor is uncertainty as to the pathways to realization proof that ideal does not lead the effort of man.

2 Stephen K. Bailey and others, *Research Frontiers in Politics and Government: Brookings Lectures, 1955* (Washington, 1955), pp. 21-22.

Law and the judiciary have their ideals, but there has been no agreement on their definition or the means of their realization. Justice indeed is the ever-present ideal, but what, as Plato queried, is justice? Is justice, for instance, equal treatment of men in unequal position or is justice protection of the claim of the weaker? The judiciary is in part an instrument of administration with an "air of detachment," as Sir Josiah Stamp said; but it is also the determiner, in the words of Pound, of the "received ideals" of the nation. How well defined are the ideals which govern the judges in this significant task? The glory of law is to some, like Pound, its certainty; for them, therefore, "a régime of law requires," as John Dickinson wrote, "a logically coherent system of general rules based on precedent and accepted principles of justice."[3] But for others the glory of law is the ever-continuing opportunity to make decisions which fit the particular circumstances, and the route to justice is freedom in a process of decision. Yet in spite of these uncertainties and differences there can be recognition that there is something more than mechanism and process and rules and standards, that there is a concept of justice which acquires reality in the decisions of man.

Is there, similarly, more than mechanism and process and more than power, in administration? Are there ideals which have acquired or may acquire reality in decision and practice? In the literature pertaining to public administration, I have found frequent reference to five ideals which are assumed to be those which should permeate its practice. These are efficiency, the rule of

[3] *Administrative Justice and the Supremacy of Law* (Cambridge, Mass., 1927), p. 113.

law, competence and responsibility, democracy, and the public interest.

These five ideals are vital parts of our national heritage. I will try in these lectures to reveal their meaning or meanings, to indicate their place in the American tradition, and to show the ways they are actually embodied or may be most effectively embodied in administrative practice. The task is similar to that of the judge as described by Cardozo: "He must balance all his ingredients, his philosophy, his logic, his analogies, his history, his customs, his sense of right, and all the rest, and adding a little here and taking out a little there, must determine, as wisely as he can, which weight shall tip the scales."[4] I can only hope that the ingredients are weighed with sufficient accuracy to make the discussion useful to those who think upon the relations between ethics and practice in government.

4 Benjamin N. Cardozo, *The Nature of the Judicial Practice* (New Haven, 1921), p. 162.

1

The Quests for Efficiency and Exact Science

EFFICIENCY IS . . . axiom number one in the value scale of administration."[1] This statement is from Luther Gulick, who probably is better qualified—on the basis of experience in the improvement of administration and in leadership in its study—to speak authoritatively of the traditions of *public* administration than any one else. There can be little doubt, also, that Gulick echoed the prevailing view of those engaged in the study and practice of public administration in this country for a full half-century—from Woodrow Wilson's famous essay introducing the subject in 1887 to Gulick's statement in 1937.[2]

From "axiom number one" Gulick has been able to state more succinctly than any other person certain corollaries as to the study of administration. It was, first, "the fundamental value upon which the science of administration may be erected." Unlike other social

[1] Luther Gulick and L. Urwick, eds., *Papers on the Science of Administration* (New York, 1937), p. 192.

[2] It is not surprising, therefore, that efficiency should have been the subject of an earlier lecture in this series. See Marshall E. Dimock, *Free Enterprise and the Administrative State* (University, Ala., 1951), Chapter IV.

sciences it was "already possible in the study of public administration" to minimize the difficulties from the intrusion of other values "by regarding all value scales as environmental with the exception of one—efficiency." Thus, the study of administration could "approximate more nearly the impersonal, valueless world in which exact science has advanced with such success."[3] Second, there was a broad unity of purpose in the study of public and business administration. Concerning the unity in the two areas Gulick has concluded: "While there are differences of objectives and emphasis, it is now clear that these are superficial, and that the underlying facts of experience are similar and complementary. It is therefore highly probable that public administration and private administration are part of a single broad science of administration. . . ."[4]

The two hopes of being a scientist and of escaping from the vagaries of politics onto the solid ground of business practice made "axiom number one" an attractive goal for students and practitioners of public administration. There were, moreover, other lures in the efficiency goal. Nothing seemed so adequately to summarize the peculiar American spirit. Efficiency has been, as Marshall Dimock has said, a kind of "religion" in the American culture, and hence, "According to American standards and values the highest compliment that a government can be paid is to be called 'efficient'."[5]

3 Gulick, in Gulick and Urwick, p. 193.

4 Gulick, "Next Steps in Public Administration," *Public Administration Review,* XV (Spring, 1955), 74.

5 Quotes from Dimock, in *Free Enterprise,* p. 124, and in John M. Gaus, Leonard D. White and Dimock, *The Frontiers of Public Administration* (Chicago, 1936), p. 116.

Also, the growth of the scientific management movement at the beginning of this century offered methodology through which the goal could be attained. Finally, the efficiency doctrine gained wide popular appeal because it was joined with the ideal of economy in government.

There developed therefore in this country the Double-E movement. The spirit of Progressivism, the revelations of the muckrakers, the new ideal of scientific management, and the formation of reform and professional organizations (the National Civil Service Reform League in 1881, the National Municipal League in 1894, and the New York Bureau of Municipal Research in 1906) led to the efficiency and economy movement, which was in the main a movement for reform on the administrative side of government. The movement started in the cities but the Double-E language gained its popular vogue from state and national studies. The Taft Economy and Efficiency Commission reported its recommendations for the national government in 1912-13, and the famous Illinois Efficiency and Economy Commission reported in 1915. Efficiency and economy became slogans of a nation desiring reform.

With the movement came a rather definite body of techniques through which the twin goals of administration could be achieved. New groups of technically qualified people arose in government and research organizations who were experts in the practice of managerial arts, through which efficiency would be attained.

Here was, in summary, goal, movement, methods, and a body of knowledge and useful art. Efficiency—the gospel of business management and an industrial culture—became the quest of public administration.

II

Efficiency has been variously defined. Until the twentieth century it seems to have been synonymous with effectiveness in achieving results, i.e. without respect to costs incurred. This is one meaning still included in dictionaries and in common discussion. An organization is said to be efficient if it produces results or if it is in readiness to produce results. But the literature of industrial and public management made men familiar with the idea that achievement of results with unnecessary expenditure of effort, time, or money was obviously inefficiency. Hence, in the literature about management more restricted definitions have been developed.

These new definitions complement each other. There are two main concepts of efficiency in the literature of scientific management. One is that of adequacy, according to which performance is measured against potentiality. Ridley and Simon state the test as follows: "The efficiency of administration is measured by the ratio of the effects actually obtained with the available resources to the maximum effects possible with the available resources."[6] It was this standard which F. W. Taylor had in mind when he laid the foundations for scientific management in his famous paper *A Piece Rate System* in 1895. He described his method of prescribing standards for job performance, and thereafter it was customary to measure the efficiency of labor by

6 Clarence Ridley and Herbert A. Simon, *Measuring Municipal Activities: A Survey of Suggested Criteria and Reporting Forms for Appraising Administration* (Chicago, 1938), p. 3.

the ratio of actual performance to the standard performance.[7] The adequacy test can also be a test of the efficiency of a service. Thus, the efficiency of fire departments has been measured by the extent to which they succeeded in reducing fire losses to the greatest extent possible.[8]

The most commonly accepted definition of efficiency, however, is in terms of a "ratio between input and output, effort and results, expenditure and income, cost and the resulting pleasure. . . ."[9] More simply stated, efficiency is measured by an input-output ratio.

Simon has concluded that for public administration the attainment of efficiency is always a relative matter and that since this is true there is no real difference between the definitions of efficiency as ratio of actual to maximum and of ratio of input to output.[10] Essentially, both call for the measurement of input against some kind of test of result. The two most commonly used definitions of efficiency are reduced to one—an input-output or resources-results relationship.

From the management approach, efficiency may be viewed also as a measure of capacity to achieve results. An organization or individual may be said to be efficient if it is in readiness to perform its task without too

[7] Sumner H. Slichter, "Efficiency," *Encyclopedia of Social Sciences* (New York, 1931), III, 437.

[8] See Ridley and Simon for analysis on fire and other departments. See also Clarence E. Ridley and Orin F. Nolting, *Check List on How Cities Can Cut Costs* (Chicago, 1949).

[9] Slichter, "Efficiency," p. 437.

[10] Herbert A. Simon, *Administrative Behavior: A Study of Decision-Making Processes in Administrative Organization* (New York, 1948), p. 181.

large an expenditure of effort. Efficiency may therefore be defined as a test of results performed *or* of readiness of an organization unit or an individual to meet demands upon it. The first is realized efficiency; the second is efficiency potential.

Efficiency is not only a test *of* administration but *for* administration. It may be a standard of judgment for the decision maker trying to decide on a course of action. As Simon says, "The criterion of efficiency dictates that choice of alternatives which produces the largest result for the given application of resources."[11]

In summary, the efficiency test may be used as

1) a measure of capacity to achieve results,
2) a measure of results attained, or
3) a standard in decision making.

Efficiency is neutral as to the content of ends or means. It does not tell us what ends are of value and is not concerned with comparison of values from alternative means, such as machines and men, which can be used in attaining ends. It only posits the ideal that results should be maximized and/or cost minimized.

The efficiency concept does, however, allow for consideration of all types of cost and all types of result. Human as well as physical costs, social as well as pecuniary results, are components in the efficiency equation. This is what we mean when we say that efficiency is not merely mechanical, physical, or monetary—that there is human efficiency, which includes cost to human beings, and social efficiency, which encompasses the total results for the community. Thus, Marshall Dimock

[11] *Ibid.*, p. 179. In italics in Simon's discussion.

has said: "If the definition of efficiency were broadened to conform to modern usage it might run something like this: Efficiency is the maximization of both the physical and the human values secured relative to the expenditures therefor, combined with the least amount of both physical and human waste."[12]

The quest for efficiency in public administration began with great emphasis on cost reduction. But this was not an essential of the efficiency ideal and was never the exclusive aim. A quantitative or qualitative improvement in results has also been part of the quest since the very beginning of the Double-E movement.

III

Efficiency was an inevitable goal of twentieth-century public administration. Improvement in organization and managerial processes was the first matter of interest in the development of the reform movement and the study of public administration. The simplest explanation of the reason for this improvement was that it would produce greater efficiency.

Structurally, administration was chaotic and confused after more than a half-century of Jacksonian democracy and a full century of inattention to principles of administrative organization. So obvious were the overlappings and duplications, and the difficulties if not impossibilities of co-ordinating related things, that common sense alone revealed certain routes to greater efficiency. Though there was some difference of opinion over the degree of integration to be sought in organiza-

12 Dimock, *Free Enterprise,* p. 147.

tion, there was no quarrel with the idea that more efficient administration could be produced by consolidation and elimination of overlapping jurisdictions. All would agree, I believe, that the result was great progress in the first half of this century in devising organization for greater efficiency.

Today the search for good organization continues. But the objectives to be sought have become more refined, the factors affecting judgment on good organization have been recognized to be more complex, and dogma has given place to the use of varied, sometimes competing, guides for building structures. Common sense answers seem no longer to be sufficient, and three new schools of thought appear: one, that organization is relatively unimportant; another, that we must develop more scientific knowledge of organization by use of new techniques of research; a third, that organization is important but is a function of good judgment based upon awareness of the facts of administrative life and the factors in a particular situation. This issue of organization has been so important that we shall devote much attention to it, albeit with respect to its service for other ends as well as that of efficiency.

Managerial processes were so poorly developed at the beginning of the century that answers here too were obvious. It is hard for the student today to comprehend the tremendous development in managerial processes over a span of two generations. Forty years ago the budget, centralized purchasing, and recruitment of personnel on the basis of merit were new goals to be achieved in the march toward efficiency. Long since, the questions have been how to refine these managerial processes to make them more useful techniques. We no longer talk about the necessity for budgeting but of the need for a performance budget and how it can be partially attained. We no longer talk about keeping the spoilsman out as the primary objective of personnel administration, but seek ways of obtaining competence and high morale. New areas of expert process are developed: administrative services has become an area of expertness, and over the past fifteen years streamlining and organization of repetitive processes has taken its place beside budget making as an important feature of the quest for efficiency.

The nation has profited greatly from the emphasis on efficiency in the drive for improved organization and management. It is impossible for me to conceive of the nation being able to wage World War II successfully or meet the peacetime challenges in recent years at national, state, and metropolitan levels without the substantial improvements in public management which had occurred as the result of the Double-E movement.

IV

If efficiency is a relationship, then use of efficiency as a route to an "exact science" assumes that it is possible to measure the relationship in a given situation. An exact science of administration based on the efficiency concept requires that input factors and output factors be isolatable and measurable. In this way judgment retroactively on the efficiency of the work of a public servant or of the performance of a unit of organization, or judgment prospectively by a decision maker on whether a course of action would be efficient, could be made with the assurance of accuracy.

Is this ideal beyond the hope of reality?

It is obvious that public administration cannot use the pecuniary standard which serves as an exact external standard for business enterprise. It may be that the test of an administrative service will be whether it avoids a deficit. But if so, this will be the result of a predetermined value judgment. In the absence of such a value judgment it would be unreasonable to conclude that a university was inefficient because tuition did not meet costs or that the postal system was inefficient because newspaper and magazine rates did not meet the cost of their handling. The first Hoover Commission found that for over fifty per cent of the purchase orders of civilian agencies of the national government, the cost of making the purchase was more than the amount of the purchase.[13] This was strong evidence that there was much inefficiency and that the source of it was in the failure to provide for co-ordinated purchasing and storage and for reduction of red tape. But even on purchasing, judgment cannot be made on the dollar test alone. Society places a high value on avoidance of fraud and favoritism in government purchases, and this may require regulations and accounting controls beyond those characteristic of private business. How far such requirements should be allowed to increase costs is an important value factor affecting judgment. Almost every report in favor of improvement in administration promises monetary savings. But this argument is more than an argument for efficiency. It assumes a value

[13] The Commission on Organization of the Executive Branch of the Government, *Office of General Services; Supply Activities* (Washington, 1949), p. 36, and *Task Force Report on the Federal Supply System* (Washington, 1949), p. 39.

judgment that reduction of cost rather than an increase in benefit is the aim of society.

There are areas of public administration in which considerable success can be and has often been achieved in measurement, but in each the limitations are considerable. One is where an engineering or physical test of efficiency is made. Where, as in construction activities, significant amounts of materials are used, efficiency requires conservation in use and engineering science provides hope for measurement of input-output factors. But a measure of public efficiency would be inadequate if it took no account of human costs—which are difficult to measure—and of the errors or successes in planning and design which would determine whether the finished product, such as a building or an instrument of warfare, would be of maximum utility to the public. Another area is the test of adequacy of city services, where comparability among jurisdictions supplies a standard of measurement. Much progress has been made in working out standards for some city departments, and these become useful in measuring the efficiency of departments in particular cities. But the measurement of efficiency by this method is rough and approximate. The factors conditioning performance vary from city to city. Qualitative differences in attainment are nonmeasurable, as is public satisfaction or dissatisfaction—which is one measure of achievement. The method has been most successful where the service is simple, standard and physical in nature, as in garbage collection; for services like health, welfare, education, and recreation it breaks down before the many imponderables of multiple objectives and human values.

An area which holds more promise for exactitude is that of repetitive processes. In recent years our O and M (Organization and Methods) technicians have served the cause of efficiency well in learning how to reduce the amount of time and the number of movements in performance of repetitive tasks. Their techniques of measurement have also been helpful as guides for organization planners and budget makers. But the strict confines of the utility of these processes are as significant as the potentialities for their use. Their utility is great where there is a single homogeneous unit of measurement, or a succession of homogeneous steps. But there are dangers in assuming homogeneity. One successful labor mediation may be more important than 1,000 minor ones. But there are other and broader limits. I recall two instances in the Office of Price Administration which illustrate both service and limitation of O and M techniques. It had been concluded on the basis of thorough study that the manpower cost in issuing rations to restaurants and other institutional users each two months could be reduced two-thirds by moving the issuance from local boards to streamlined issuance centers in district offices. Many objected that the move would be unwise. They believed that the withdrawal of issuance from local boards would cause inconvenience to institutional users and much loss of good will in the communities. The change was made, but only after careful plans to minimize the inconvenience and loss of good will. In the other instance, co-operative task forces from the Bureau of the Budget and OPA had made extensive time checks on the operations at desks of all professional and clerical personnel in rationing in selected district offices. They had calculated for the 57 program actions, for the several types of public relations tasks, and for other activities at the food chiefs' desks the number of items to be handled over a period of time and had estimated the average time for each; and had done the same for all the other desks. On the basis of this they had advised substantial changes in personnel and budget allocations. In a succeeding conference the head of the department appropriately raised the question as to whether personnel and budget allocations could be determined primarily on the basis of mathematical calculations. In the end again the recommendations were in general followed, though with much adjustment as a result of consideration of program priorities and of the judgments of supervisory personnel and the persons carrying on the professional tasks.

There is nothing unusual in these examples. They do illustrate the conclusion that even when measurable aspects of administration are extensive, wisdom in decision calls for awareness of and judgment on factors outside the area of measurement.

Yet experience with desk audits and measurement of repetitive processes gives a very partial revelation of the limitations on measurement—either by the decision maker in administration or by those who judge his decisions. Burkhead, in his recent book *Government Budgeting,* has noted certain difficulties on the output side of the efficiency equation. He finds that "definable, homogeneous, and significant end products do not exist in many cases." It is useless, he says, "to search for a homogeneous end-product unit that will measure 'better education', 'better defense', or 'more economic and efficient personnel recruitment'." He concludes that it is an "illusion that program content and accomplishment can be measured by the discrete things that are done by government," and that end-product classifications "cannot measure performance in any value sense."[14]

Value attainments must be the measure of administration, but values are not the subject of exact science. Values cannot be measured in concrete terms. There are no common denominators of value, by which one can measure whether administrators should give more money to education or to health, or more money to one health function than another, or divert money to the education of the upper quartile in college. Distributive values—who among competing claimants among the groups in society should receive benefits?—create especially difficult problems.[15]

It is evident, therefore, that on the output side the administrator makes qualitative judgments among competing considerations of value. He must also make value judgments on the input side of the efficiency equation. For example, in deciding whether to substitute machines for men he must consider the claims of the latter for softened impact of change. Value considerations may be more important than pure efficiency considerations. As a strict conformer to the principle of efficiency the administrator might decide that a rest period twice a day would result in more production. But he might be led to favor a rest period by an assumption that employees should be treated humanely. The dig-

14 Jesse Burkhead, *Government Budgeting* (New York and London, 1956), pp. 139-43.

15 See Simon, *Administrative Behavior,* pp. 175-78.

nity and value of man may often be an acceptable reason in the administrator's mind for personnel actions on which he has made no quantitative analysis.

V

The greatest deficiency of the efficiency goal is not that efficiency is nonmeasurable but that the goal itself is inadequate.

The input-output test is inadequate because there are other elements in decision making besides the means-end relationship.

This may be quickly illustrated with a few examples. The Federal Trade Commission makes a decision on whether a concern has violated the legal prohibition against an unfair method of competition. This involves a judgment on whether certain facts revealed in a hearing constitute violation. There is no input-output situation here unless the time and cost of the trial be measured; but the time and cost of the trial is no test of the good judgment in the decision. The Federal Reserve Board makes a decision to raise the discount rate. In doing so it balances anticipated losses and gains on the result side only. The input of time and cost in making the decision is of small moment, if not completely insignificant, as compared with the quality of the judgment of public consequences. The young foreign service officer in the Indonesian Assignment case had to decide whether to contact the Republican government for information or restrict his inquiries to the Dutch. He had good reason to believe that his superior preferred the latter, but his loyalty to good professional service told him that the former was desirable. His decision was a result—among other things which we need not discuss—of the weighing of values and of a determination between conflicting loyalties.

The input-output factor is, therefore, a quite inconsequential one in much decision making. The efficiency goal as defined in management literature can have little or no value when the decision is primarily an application of a legal standard to facts, balancing of consequences, or choice among values or loyalties.

The efficiency goal is of more value as a test of government on the management side than of government on the policy making side. But there is great truth in James Landis' statement after experience on three regulatory commissions that the ultimate test of administration is "in the policy that it formulates"[16] and in Gulick's statement in this lecture series that "translation from purpose to program is the crucial step in administration."[17]

The making of public policy may be the most complex of human undertakings. The policy maker must consider the reactions of others, particularly in foreign affairs, but also in domestic affairs. He must often take account of the complex interaction of multiple forces and institutional factors. His decision is a judgment in which assessment of conditions, value assumptions, and human reactions all become significant. The means-ends construct is relatively meaningless for such a function.

16 James Landis, *The Administrative Process* (New Haven, 1938), p. 39.

17 Gulick, *Administrative Reflections from World War II* (University, Ala., 1948), p. 78.

It is possible that the management concept of efficiency has now become so inadequate as a measure of the total process of government that the term "efficiency" should be redefined. It might include success in balancing results as well as success in achieving a satisfactory means-result ratio. It might include skill in applying law to facts. It might include skill in tracing all aspects of a problem and defining the alternatives of solution which are feasible. It might, in other words, be once again accepted as merely effective performance. For an agency itself it might mean getting a job done well.

This broader concept, like the input-output relationship, would provide one good test of administration. But even the broader concept would not supply a completely adequate test for administration in areas where it is recipient of discretionary responsibilities. What is the job to be done? Is this clear for the Federal Reserve Board? For the Civil Aeronautics Board? In general, yes; in specific, no. How much of the job is to be done, i.e., what level of attainment is to be sought? Is this clear for the Federal Trade Commission? What is to be sacrificed in doing the job? Whose ox can be gored with how much blood-letting? Whose benefit is to be sought and with what reservations? When loyalties are in conflict, which are to be given priority?

These questions emphasize the basic inadequacy of the efficiency goal. However defined, whether as a means-end relationship or merely as effectiveness in producing results, it gives the administrator no guide for choice among values. The administrator is no automaton with all guides for action laid out. Statute and other overhead directives often provide general and vague, perhaps even conflicting guides, either or both on means and ends. They may even leave him with no guide at all. He may have to find his lead for action in the general nature of his program. Or he may find that program objectives must be balanced with community ideals.

The scope of this search for controlling values may be illustrated by a couple of examples. A military commander may have a clear military objective of winning a battle, but winning it may involve great sacrifice of human life. More human material may be readily available but the commander may still consider the sacrifice too great. Why should he? Because the society he represents is permeated with the ideal of the value of each and every life. I recall a conference in the public service in which I argued that we were concerned in our enforcement efforts only with the "solvency of our program." A fellow bureaucrat protested, "Hell, no! We are interested in the solvency of the system of law." I was interested in getting a job done, as defined in program objectives; he was interested in the effects of the performance of our job on the survival of community values. I readily admit that his was the broader and the more correct vision. No administrator has the right to adopt expedients which save his program but impair the values upon which the success of all public functions depends.

We have reached this position: efficiency is measurable only in terms of the attainment of all community ideals which the administrator is obligated by his official and moral nature to consider, yet the efficiency test provides no guide for measuring these ideals. This has important implications for training for the public service. It means that the public administrator should know more than the techniques necessary for efficiency. Quite obviously he must know also the definition of purpose prescribed for his function in law and regulation. This, however, is a function of in-service training. Beyond this he should know the ideals of society toward which efficiency techniques are to be directed. He should have deep appreciation and feeling for the cultural traditions of his society. This may be obtained in part in courses in political science revealing the public philosophy of Western culture but it seems to require study in a more diverse literature. It was appropriate for Professor Finer in a book on training of nurses in administration to include an appendix listing suggestions for humanistic reading.[18]

VI

A science which measured only actions and stopped short of the vital process of decision making would not be a science of administration but only of parts of administration. Decision making in administration has been ably analyzed by Herbert Simon, leader among the advocates of a scientific study of administration in a new generation. Simon concludes that there are value judgments and factual judgments in decisions.[19]

18 Herman Finer, *Administration and the Nursing Services* (New York, 1952).

19 Simon, *Administrative Behavior*, pp. 4-5, and "'Development of Theory of Democratic Administration'; Replies and Comments," *American Political Science Review*, XLVI (June, 1952), 494-96.

The former are statements of ethical preference, the latter are "statements about the observable world and the way in which it operates."[20] Only the latter is the area for a science of administration. Efficiency, Simon says, is the criterion within this area. It is now defined as "the criterion which the administrator applies to factual problems."[21]

Simon believes, however, that "separation between the ethical and the factual elements in judgment can usually be carried only a short distance."[22] This would seem to block the attempt to make administration a science, but Simon does not despair. He distinguishes between ultimate and intermediary ends, the latter being means with relation to the former and therefore "factual questions." To apply science in administration requires that intermediary goals be stated and given "relative weights."[23]

This may be a desirable part of the process of analysis, but is it always feasible? Who would believe that the process of stating relative weights for intermediary goals could be that of an exact science? One impediment would be the difficulty of separating ultimate and intermediary goals, for what is intermediary to one man is ultimate to another. Moreover, intermediary ends cannot be set until there is a statement of ultimate ends. It seems that Donald Kingsley was right: "A 'science' of means is a possible adventure only in a stable social en-

20 Simon, *Administrative Behavior,* p. 45; also p. 248.
21 *Ibid.,* p. 186.
22 *Ibid.,* p. 52.
23 *Ibid.,* pp. 53, 176.

vironment in which the effective political elements accept a common ideology and a common scale of values."[24]

Simon has jumped from a definition of efficiency in its traditional meaning of an input-output relationship to one where it is a measure of all factual relationships. But even then he has reduced the test of efficiency and the goal of an "exact science" of administration to something less than a full test of administrative performance. The administrator must make value judgments; as to these the efficiency criterion must be neutral.[25] The administrator must make judgments where the value assumptions are not strictly definable; in such cases the efficiency criterion cannot take hold or can do so imperfectly. Simon has, like Gulick, sought to eliminate other value tests besides efficiency, but in his realistic restriction of the measurement of efficiency to factual matters he has seriously restricted the area in which we may anticipate an approach toward "exact science." The most that can be said is that there are elements in public administration which are measurable and that for this reason we can expect, as Gulick hopes, to go further in the development of science in this area than in the social sciences generally. In fact, the student and practitioner of administration, noting the great progress in managerial science and in the study of the sociology of administration, can argue confidently that this already has been true in significant measure.

24 In a book review, *Public Administration Review,* V (Winter, 1945), 88.

25 Simon agrees. *Administrative Behavior,* p. 14.

VII

Efficiency is undoubtedly one of the axioms of good administration. So vast a proportion of the physical and human assets of society is expended through public administration that efficiency in the employment of these assets is a test not alone of government but of the total utility of the nation's effort. It is more important today than when the Double-E movement started that public money and human effort employed in the public service be productive of results. It is essential that organization and processes of government continue to be fashioned toward the realization of efficiency and that public servants be trained to be efficient.

Yet efficiency can never be the only test of administration. Efficiency is a test of a means-ends relationship or of ability to achieve ends, but not a test for measuring consequences or choosing ends. It can be a test for administration only to the extent that administration itself is solely of instrumental significance. Conversely, to the extent that administration becomes *balancer of consequences and selector among ends,* then the efficiency criterion collapses.

The study of public administration was built initially upon the argument, first made by Woodrow Wilson in the essay which inaugurated the study,[26] that public administration was an instrument only. Wilson and his contemporary, Professor Frank Goodnow, supplied the students of administration with the assumption that the

26 Woodrow Wilson, "The Study of Administration," *Political Science Quarterly,* II (June, 1887), 197-222, reprinted in LXI (December, 1941), 481-506.

determination of the content or substance of policy could be made by political officials and that administration would be only the arrangements for implementing policies. On the conveyor belt of implementation, policy would be served but not modified.

This neat dichotomy does not describe the realities of twentieth century administration. Definition of ends and purposes is not completed in the political structure; the ends of government, though perhaps generally defined in political directives, are elaborated in administrative decision. Even selection of means of implementation involves new policy judgments in which value considerations weigh heavily. And through budgeting, recommendation of legislation, and advice to the chief executive and legislatures, administration influences basic value determinations in the political branches of the government.

The study of public administration must deal with the total process of administration. It will be incomplete if built upon concepts which fit only the input-output relationship, the factual part of a factual-ethical complex, the quantitative elements in a quantitative-qualitative function, the neutral aspects of a neutral-purposeful mixture.

The basic values to be sought are those of society; they are cultural values. Some of these are leading guides for business as well as government and hence present opportunities for "a single broad" study of public and business administration. Efficiency is, of course, one of these. The dignity of man is another. That ideal is accepted in personnel management in business—indeed the lead has often been taken in business administration. In part then, the ideals of business and public administration are the same and the "underlying facts of experience" in the two are, as Gulick said, "similar and complementary." This is the area for what Dwight Waldo calls "structural-functional analysis," which puts emphasis on similarities in all areas of administration.[27]

Yet the differences between the two appear to me to be more than "superficial." Even the concepts of efficiency and the dignity of man may be affected in application by the different cultural climates of business and government. More significant, there are other value concepts which are peculiar features of a *public* philosophy. These value concepts may have real significance in economic affairs, but their impact in government is distinctly different. Three of these are the concepts of supremacy of law, the public interest, and democracy. These elements in the public philosophy are topics of succeeding chapters.

27 *The Study of Public Administration* (Garden City, N. Y., 1955), p. 9.

2

The Rule of Law Versus the Discretion of Men

HARRINGTON'S FAMOUS PHRASE, "a government of laws," summarizes the most persistent political ideal of Western civilization. Aristotle grappled with the question of whether a government of laws or of men would be superior and drew a conclusion which would have been acceptable to Cicero, medieval thinkers, Coke, Harrington, and the American founding fathers, that "he who would place the supreme power in mind, would place it in God and the laws."[1] John of Salisbury saw it as an issue between force and law, which in our day has often been patently presented in the relations among races and nations, and of labor to employer, and of people to government. Harrington summarized the old ideal in words which could become creed to guide Americans in their constitution making, to the end, as the Massachusetts Constitution of 1780 said, that we might have "a government of laws and not of men."

In our own peculiar development—in part European, in part indigenous—five major types of embellishment were added to the basic ideal. The first was in the de-

1 *Politics,* Book III, Chapter 16 (Everyman's ed., 1912).

velopment of types of positive law, of which there were three. The first of these was the law of judges, which according to Chief Justice Fortescue and others was discovered by them out of natural equity and custom. The second was the law made by legislatures and interpreted in particular cases in the courts. And the third was the law made by sovereign people, embodied in constitutions and again interpreted by the courts. Whatever the source, all three, after Marshall, ran back to the courts as interpreters and declarers of the law.

The second embellishment was the idea that the rule of law could be preserved by the separation of powers. This idea had its origins in continental struggles but was given its consummate expression in the Massachusetts Constitution of 1780. The English, as the text of Bracton puts it, sought "to put a bridle" on the king. The Americans, after a bit of experience with legislative supremacy under the first state constitutions, sought an institutional framework through which bridles would be put on all organs of government. This was the function of separation of powers and the accompanying principle of checks and balances.

The third embellishment is as old as the idea of the supremacy of law, and some would think it an essential to the idea. It is the idea that there is a law beyond man—a higher law which limits all government, whether of kings or of people. This is the law of God or the law of His creation—nature. "True law," declared Cicero, "is right reason consonant with nature, diffused among all men, constant, eternal. . . ."[2]

[2] *De Re Publica,* ed. C. F. W. Mueller (Leipsic, 1910), III, 22, quoted in Charles Howard McIlwain, *The Growth of Political Thought in the West* (New York, 1932), p. 111.

In Anglo-American history the idea of a higher law has struggled with the idea of the supremacy of the positive law. In the early seventeenth century, before the idea of sovereignty was generally recognized, Coke defended the supremacy of judge-made law over the claims of king and Parliament by setting up the idea that the common law was the protector of "common right and reason." And when near the end of the same century the legal supremacy of Parliament had been established, Locke argued that Parliament itself was limited by the natural law.

In America this idea that the sovereignty of legislatures was limited by a higher law first found expression in claims of natural right, then got embodied in written constitutions, which could limit legislatures as well as executives. This development then presented another area of conflict between natural law and positive law. Two basic principles of the Declaration of Independence stood in apparent conflict: the one that inalienable rights of men limited government, the other that government derived its "just powers from the consent of the governed." Which was the higher principle: higher law or popular sovereignty? Were the people themselves bound by a higher law?

The fourth embellishment was the idea of judicial review. As Marshall explained it, this was support for popular sovereignty, for the constitution enforced by the Court emanated from the people. But Marshall, in Fletcher v. Peck in 1810, also suggested that there might be extraconstitutional limits in the "general principles which are common to our free institutions," and the constitution itself was sufficiently flexible to give the judges opportunity to write into it their own views of "common right and reason." Thus, it appeared that perhaps neither separation of powers nor popular sovereignty was the supreme principle, but rather judicial supremacy. This might be defended as Coke did in his fight with James I on the basis of the claim that only those with a special type of esoteric wisdom gained by study of the law were equipped to determine it, or as Marshall did in Marbury v. Madison on the grounds of jurisdiction, but in either case law was what the courts said it was.

It can be seen that the concept of the rule of law has had several meanings. It has meant that man should govern through law (the ideal of positive law), that man was limited by law (the ideal of higher law), that no man or group alone should determine and apply the law (the concept of separation of powers), and that law was what judges said it was (a concept of judicial supremacy). These concepts are not all concordant. And beyond the discordancies of the past, there has arisen the modern conflict between traditionalists and realists, the first finding the value of law in its rules, standards, and concepts and the certainty they offer, the latter regarding law as the process by which correct answers are found for litigated issues. "Rule of law," in sum, cannot be defined precisely and singly, and consequently discussion of it must carry along several notions for contrast or comparison with the free judgment or discretion of man.

All of this has relevance for administration, but I am immediately interested in a fifth type of embellishment which affected administration directly. Here three things have been significant. The first was the development in England of the jurisdiction of the courts over administration. By the great writs which the courts could issue to officers, and by the subjection of officers to civil and criminal liability, the judiciary was able to enforce all types of positive law over officers in the executive branch. Thus we have had judicial review, exercised in the regular courts, over administration. Second, when legislative power was established in Parliament, Locke said that one limitation on Parliament was that it could not delegate its legislative power. This idea, which was accepted in political theory in this country, meant that administration could not make but could only carry out law. Third, as modern legislation began to make grants of discretion to administrative officers the courts claimed a right of reviewability of administrative decisions. For the old idea that only the courts should apply the law in specific cases, there was now substituted the idea that administrators could apply the law subject to correction by the courts.

The result of all of this was to confine the administrative function and hold administration under the ideal of the rule of law. The result also was, if not to make administration a completely neutral function, at least to keep it from being a disturbing, or a socially creative, one. It got its direction from law, it was held in check by law, it of all government functions had the least effect upon things, and if it was merely efficient man need have no further serious concern about it.

II

There have been three modern developments in government which have qualified the effects upon administration of these elements of embellishment upon the idea of the rule of law.

The first of these has been the actual fact and the legal recognition of delegation of "legislative" power. In a time when Congress is unable to legislate in detail on the many matters before it, the Supreme Court has said that "the Constitution . . . does not demand the impossible or the impracticable."[3] As Corwin has said, "Congress is enabled to delegate its powers whenever it is necessary and proper to do so in order to exercise them effectively."[4] The necessity has been recognized also in the states. In fact, as long ago as 1908, the New York Court of Appeals presaged modern developments when it suggested a statute might be void if it prescribed any other rule for an administrative commission fixing rates except the general standard of reasonableness.[5] Today the policy-making power of legislatures is regularly delegated and the enormous extent of the delegation of discretion to administrative agencies has been revealed in a number of major decisions, like those in the Rock Royal, Yakus, and Lichter cases. Legislation inaugurates and confines programs, but it does not define their full content. This is the function of administration. In discharging the function, administration becomes a new source of positive law, and thus a subordinate law-making power is concentrated in each of many agencies of administration and exercised, by and large, beyond the reach of the principle of separation of powers.

The second is the union of functions in administra-

[3] Yakus v. U.S., 321 U.S. 414, 424 (1944).

[4] E. S. Corwin, *The Twilight of the Supreme Court* (New Haven, 1934), pp. 144-45.

[5] Village of Saratoga Springs v. Saratoga Gas, Electric Light and Power Co., 83 N.E. 693, 700.

tive agencies. Today they exercise, along with executive functions, judicial and legislative powers—"softened only by a quasi," as Justice Holmes said of legislative power. They become, through law-making and law-interpretation functions, a fourth source of positive law. The general practice of legislatures today is to overlook, as aptly phrased by James Landis, the "triadic contours" of separation of powers and delegate to the same agency all the powers related to the discharge of a function.

Third, the courts have to a very substantial extent lost control over administration. This I think has come about largely for three reasons. For one thing, administration has become of such vast extent and handles so many particulars that it is necessary for it to set up organization and procedure to dispose of the great bulk of nondisputed and disputed matters *within its own house*. An example is the Internal Revenue Service where a system of appeals within the agency eliminates and settles most disputed issues, so that few move on to the courts. Many are settled by compromise and most are settled by a procedure which is much simpler and less time-consuming than formal judicial procedure. For administration affecting millions of people—whether it be internal revenue, social security, or selective service—the challenge is for organization under which most business is sifted out in the early stages of a procedural hierarchy.

In addition, the courts have found it impossible to take hold of new functions of administration. The courts, by their own definition of jurisdiction, have shut themselves out of such things as the actual setting of rates or granting of licenses. Rate-making is legislative, licensing is administrative, say the courts, and hence these and all other functions similarly defined are inappropriate for judicial action in national and most state jurisdictions. The courts can pass on what others have done, or remand for another decision, but they cannot in many instances determine themselves the action to be taken. Not only can they not perform because of legal limits; but for practical reasons they cannot correct many things in administration which would adversely affect man's rights. They cannot correct laxness, force constructive planning, nor—even though the Administrative Procedure Act authorizes it—effectively prevent delays which would injure private parties or the public interest. They cannot affect certain major decisions of the Treasury or the Federal Reserve Board or force the President to make or not to make a trade agreement. Examples could be multiplied but those given are sufficient to illustrate that the judicial net over administration is full of holes.

Finally, new forms of esoteric wisdom have been required for informed judgment on the issues of the time. Three and a half centuries ago in a great struggle between the courts and the king, James I claimed the quality of "natural reason," and Coke answered that the law was "an artificial perfection of reason, gotten by long study, observation and experience." This was a struggle between common sense and expert sense, and Coke's claim for the eggheads with expert sense has through the course of history won a substantial measure of vindication. The issue of the twentieth century has been different. Listen to Justice Frankfurter in oil proration cases in which the Supreme Court refused to set aside orders of the Texas Railroad Commission: the claims of the parties were "enmeshed in a conflict of expertise"; "accommodation of conflicting private interests" is "beset with perplexities, both geological and economic"; the judicial process is adaptable "only to issues definitely circumscribed and susceptible of being judged by the techniques and criteria within the special competence of lawyers"; the administrative agency "presumably . . . possesses an insight and aptitude."[6] This was a struggle between "jack-of-all-wisdom" and functional expertness, and in this struggle the functional experts have been winning. "True law" may be, as Cicero said, "right reason"; but it is often now the right reason of administrative experts seeking a rule for new and changing situations.

The result of these modern developments has been to expand the place of administration in government. Legislatures delegate, all types of powers are placed in the same agency, the courts withdraw. As a consequence, the old issue of the rule of law vs. the discretion of men is presented again. Whereas it has been debated in the past primarily with respect to kings, parliaments and peoples, it may now be focused on the multiple and diverse recipients of responsibility for program development and policy formation. We may appropriately examine the role of law and the role of discretion for administration. Let us look first at one side of the coin, then at the other.

III

It would be a mistake to conclude that the modifications in the doctrines of nondelegability, separation of powers, and judicial review have destroyed the effect of

6 Railroad Commission v. Rowan & Nichols Co., 310 U.S. 573, 582 (1940); 311 U.S. 570, 574-76 (1941).

the great ideal of the rule of law on administration. The ideal need not be confused with all of its embellishments, which as we have seen are not all concordant. The basic ideal has worked itself into the practice of government in new ways and through extensions of old methods.

In describing these developments, I should note in the beginning that administration has actually provided an instrument for the expansion of law in our society. As new law has been needed for grazing on public lands, for stock exchanges, for civil aeronautics, or for allocation of scarce resources in wartime, Congress has bestowed the rule-making power on administrative agencies. And as new law was needed for trade practices and for labor practices, Congress has set up broad guiding standards and chosen administration as the instrument for elaborating these standards in case-to-case administration. Thus Congress is provided with practical means for the development of law, either through the legislative technique of rule making or the judicial technique of case-to-case decision.

There was no disappearance of the rule of law in society because equity jurisdiction developed as a parallel to common law courts, or because legislatures arose as a supplement to both. There is no necessary disappearance of the rule of law because a fourth arm is added to the former triumvirate of law-making jurisdictions. There is always fear of the new, but where ideal is strong it will permeate the new as it has the old.

One permeation is the application of due process. A basic ingredient of substantive due process is the avoidance of arbitrary and discriminatory action. For the administrator who must deal with many individuals, there is a natural impulse to adhere unflinchingly to this standard. It is the core of integrity of the program he administers and of his own official conduct. In organizations of size there will be checks within the organization which enforce obedience to the standard. Among these are the need for many to concur in decisions, the influence of lawyers and other professionals in the organization, the desire of each official to be regarded by his fellow workers as a person with official integrity, and the rules of practice which govern the application of policy to particular cases.

The process of administrative decision is engirded in procedural due process. This is only in part a result of the rules of good practice developed for rule making and adjudication as now embodied in the Administrative Procedure Act and similar acts in many of the states. Procedural due process in administration involves much more. It includes all the arrangements for obtaining information on the prospective effects of decisions and for the internal pooling of knowledge from the various types of experts within an agency.

One of the most common misconceptions about administration is that decisions are made by individual men. This is only rarely true, save only for those cases now decided by examiners. Decision in large organizations is a composite of wisdom from many sources. No judicial opinion which has come to my attention shows such immense ignorance of this fact as that of Justice Roberts in the famous wartime rent case where he said it was "plain" that the statute created "personal government by a petty tyrant instead of government by law" and that the effectiveness, scope, etc. of the rent order were matters "buried in the bosom of the administrator and nowhere else."[7] The eminent justice seemed not to realize that there was a very elaborate process within the agency for considering these matters, in which the wisdom of persons inside and outside the administration was tapped, and that the head of the agency may not even have participated at all in the decision. Nor did he seem to realize that where decisions of broad policy affecting many people are made, the realities of due process will be safeguarded most effectively by the process of institutional decision.

Rule making is another means by which the ideal of rule of law permeates administration. In a special report for the President's Committee on Administrative Management (1937) James Hart discussed rule making as "a satisfactory middle term between legislation and final adjudication." Through this "middle term" the traditional concept of the rule of law could be maintained. He redefined the concept of rule of law:

> That idea can no longer mean the rule of detailed statutes. It means rather, first, that Congress should guide the administrator by as careful a definition of general policy as is possible, and, second, that the gap between congressional mandate and administrative orders in particular cases be bridged, though by no means narrowed to mere red tape, by the rule-making power.[8]

In addition to the making of rules applicable to the general public the administrative agencies have found

7 Dissenting in Bowles v. Willingham, 321 U.S. 503, 537 (1944).

8 President's Committee on Administrative Management, *Report with Special Studies* (Washington, 1937), p. 326.

many ways of developing a rule of law to govern operations within their several organizations. They have developed, as it were, law *for* their respective organizations. And in so doing they have matched origination out of the science and art of administration with the new demands on government, to the end that order and consistency could prevail. In hierarchical organizations there must be a system of order so that men may be held to uniform ways of acting. So there develops an internal law for the organization, which includes the internal substantive and procedural standards which fix or guide the conduct of persons within the hierarchy.

This may be illustrated with some examples. The Post Office Department conducts a program where operating, as contrasted with policy, decisions are made through a vast organization of nearly 40,000 post offices. For nearly all questions which arise a postmaster can find his answers in the standards prescribed in one thick Postal Manual. He follows it scrupulously and carefully. In wartime rationing a similar system was used for local rationing boards, and the boards developed the idea, "The green book is the Bible." During World War II as programs developed rapidly much discretion was necessarily left in early days with those who had to face new problems. In the southwestern region laundry price adjustments had to be made before the national office could develop standards. The regional office in the first two adjustments fixed uniform prices for all laundries in each of two cities. This flat-pricing pattern fitted the past practice in those cities. Then a case arose where laundries in the city had varying prices for laundry services, and the regional office made adjustments for each laundry separately. In the first two cases, after telephone conversation with the Washington office, the regional office allowed a seven per cent return on gross receipts, but by the third case it and the national office had agreed that eight per cent was fairer. At this stage the national office developed a set of instructions providing for individual adjustments and an eight per cent return, and detailing the accounting methods to be used. This set of instructions became the guide, then the binding rule of the organization, and ultimately was made available to laundry operators. Of more significance was the elaboration of standards in the same agency to guide the framers of price regulations. The general language of the statute was supplemented by policy standards developed in the top administrative offices. Each division of the organization became familiar with these standards, some of which in time were given legal force by approval in the Emergency Court of Appeals.

Thus, a distinct type of legalization arises: rules to govern the ways of subordinates in a hierarchical structure. These rules are enforced by a variety of techniques. One is the system of internal appeals, now often so judicialized in process as to resemble the method by which deviation from standard by lower courts is corrected in the judiciary. Another method is the preaudit or clearance of decision by a superior. Still another is the postaudit of actions taken. The most common method is to make these rules of internal policy part of the custom of the organization through the system of communication and the development of loyalty of personnel to the hierarchical system. Whatever the battery of techniques, there always develops within a large organization a system of checks to insure that the internal legal order is maintained.

The internal law for each organization is supplemented by the external law *controlling* administrative organizations generally. This is administrative law in its broadest sense. Some of it relates to finance—the rules concerning budgeting, purchasing, accounting, use of appropriations, and audits. Some of it relates to personnel, for which a considerable amount of legal protection has developed. Some of it relates to procedure in rule making and adjudication and is embodied in the Administrative Procedure Act, other acts of Congress, and legislation of the states. Some of it is contained in judicial rules on due process, on discriminatory and arbitrary action, and on other matters on which the courts hold a ring around administration. On these several types of things the agencies are kept on guard at all times by finance officers, personnel officers, the ubiquitous agency lawyers, and more remotely, by the courts.

Added to all of this is the fact that Congress has not abdicated its legislative function. On the contrary, Congress has continued to legislate in areas in which it has delegated its power. To an extent, a co-operative relationship has developed between the agencies and the Congress in the development of law. The agencies, as the functional experts in areas of government policy, have recommended legislation to Congress. Professor Sharfman concluded in his monumental study of the Interstate Commerce Commission that "while the Congressional response has often been tardy, it has seldom swerved, in essence, from the direction of the Commission's recommendations."[9] In other cases conflict develops between the Congress and the agencies, with the result that Congress amends its earlier enactments. This was the case, for example, with OPA during World War II. Each time the governing statute on price control was extended the Congress added more detail and more modification of administrative policies. Sometimes the center of law making shifts like moves on a checkerboard among the three branches. This has been the case with natural gas regulation, where the Federal Power Commission ruled it did not have jurisdiction over a company like the Phillips Petroleum Co., the Supreme Court ruled it did, the Congress by law said it should not, and the President vetoed the congressional act. It appears that sometimes policy is only effective if all branches of the government are for it, and that the separation of powers principle still operates as a guarantee that no single group will make the law.

Charles Hyneman has stated a significant conclusion about the continuing participation of Congress in development of program law:

> This is the history of a great part of our legislation. In the initial period of regulation, Congress is forced to abdicate to the administrator for the extension of policy beyond the statement of general purposes. As time passes and administrative experience is examined, Congress is able to incorporate into statute the policies formulated and pursued by the administrative department.[10]

[9] I. L. Sharfman, *The Interstate Commerce Commission* (New York, 1931), I, 290.

[10] *Bureaucracy in a Democracy* (New York, 1950), pp. 88-89.

Experience further shows that Congress is selective among the policies of agencies, perpetuating some, conditioning or overruling others.

Whether Congress acts will depend on whether new authorizations are needed for administration or on whether the interests affected by administration are satisfied with its performance. If they are not and find no relief in the courts, they are likely to turn to the Congress. The administrative agency may begin its work with a broad and general statute and soon find it is still subject to the attention, check, and new directive of the Congress.

It appears then that law reigns in many ways. Administrators are bridled men, and many of the bridles are legal.

IV

Though administration is permeated and circumscribed by law, discretion is vital to its performance.

It is well to recognize at the outset of a discussion of discretion that it is not peculiar to administration nor to recent practice. It would be misleading, for example, to talk about the enforcement of criminal justice without recognizing that, parallel to the concept of law, there is the idea of escape from the rigor of law. Part of this escape is provided within, part outside the courts. It is allowable at four stages: the examining and prosecuting stage, where the grand jury may not bill or the prosecutor may neglect to press a case; the jury decision on guilt or innocence, where leniency may replace the strict requirement of law; the assessment of penalties, where judge or jury may vary the penalty—perhaps even with discretion ranging all the way from death to probation; and at the executive clemency stage—remnant of the old prerogative of the crown to mitigate the severity and perhaps the injustice of the law. Mercy, influence or social position, and belief in a justice higher than the letter of the law become factors in the substitution of discretion for strict application of the law. It may be that this process has gone too far—that for example we need an appellate process for equalizing sentences, particularly where these are assessed by juries as in state courts in my state—but no one would seriously urge that law alone should govern in this process.

It would be misleading also to talk about the rule of law without recognizing that courts have moderated the positive law of legislatures by their own concepts of reason. Interpretation of the antitrust laws is, of course, the most glaring example. The rule of reason in antitrust cases has preserved for the courts continuous discretion as to what is legal and what is illegal. This does not mean, I hasten to add, that the discretion is unlimited, but only that it is large. Yet even more can be said. A judicial veto over the content of legislation has in fact been exercised under the guise of interpretation. How else, for example, can one explain the gutting of the original Section 7 of the Clayton Act in the decisions of the Supreme Court?

Did judicial supremacy on valuation from 1890 to 1944 bring a rule of law? The prescription of the Minnesota Rate case of 1913 that "there should be a proper consideration of all relevant facts,"[11] supplemented by the leanings toward reproduction cost in later years,

[11] Simpson v. Shepard, 230 U.S. 352, 434.

never gave administrators an adequate or workable standard and established only a continuing discretion in the courts to torpedo whatever administrative craft seemed to be on the wrong course. And when the Supreme Court changed its mind on all of this in 1944 it again gave no definite standard of judgment. It accepted rather the philosophy of pragmatism for this matter: rates must be judged by the "end result," and this would be determined by balancing the interests of investors and consumers.[12]

I think we find in these limitations of the rule of law in the judiciary two clues to an understanding of why discretion is characteristic of administration: law is rigid, and policy must be made pragmatically.

The rigor of a regime of law is constantly mitigated by administrative agencies. Those which have power to impose or initiate sanctions reserve the severe sanctions provided by law for application to the willful, fraudulent, flagrant, or repeated violator. They may develop their own scale of softer measures for other types of violation. They may even overlook many violations as merely unavoidable leakage in the administrative system. By administrative necessity, or by the claims of justice, they may be led to pick from among many instances of violation those which will be prosecuted in administrative, civil, or criminal proceedings.

But the concessions to discretion are greater. I cite two examples out of wartime experience. The head of the War Production Board set up a method for making grants of scarce commodities outside of the regulations.

12 Federal Power Commission v. Hope Natural Gas Co., 320 U.S. 591 (1944).

He vested in a board the power to make determinations within its own discretion, which has been called the placing of the conscience of the agency in the hands of a board. The other example is in local board administration of rationing. The boards were bound by rules on who could receive gasoline and in what amounts. They thought some of the rules were too rigid; they sometimes violated the rules, as for example in granting gasoline to go to funerals. The agency finally found a compromise between rule and discretion. It granted each board a small quota of so-called "hardship" gasoline which it could distribute according to its own conscience. Who can say that the law of a central agency is always better than the conscience of the person who stands on the firing line to administer a program?

There are, of course, instances where rules of law are found to be unjust because they are insufficiently tailored to variable circumstance. In such an event some route to exception must be found. For example, during the war the price control agency used several routes: adjustments for particular sellers, special rules for pricing new merchandise, amendments to regulations. All of this, if done under prescribed rule applicable to all in like circumstances retains the rule of law; but the point of emphasis is that administration may be in a good position to use discretion in the modification and refinement of rules so that justice may be particularized.

In administration, however, the most significant departures from or adaptations of the rule of law are not those related to the mitigation of severity of law or to adjustments to insure greater justice. One of the areas of greatest difficulty is in the grant or denial of business opportunities. The public works contract has been an everpresent threat to the efficiency and purity of government. The evils of discretion in this area have been fought by the device of competitive bidding. But the device is not always usable, as in many military and atomic energy contracts where judgment on special competence, plant facilities, ability to deliver on time, and other needs may affect the judgment of the administrator awarding contracts.[13] Similarly, discretionary judgments are made on the grant of such valuable privileges as radio and television licenses and air routes. In these areas, where such large opportunities exist for private gain and for sacrifice of public interests, it would appear to be desirable to seek continuously to narrow the range of discretion through development of policy standards.

But the largest departure from the ideal of rule of law is in the making and changing of policy. Much of administrative policy making is not refinement of general statute into standing administrative rules; it is decision for the day on the situation which exists and may be modified as the situation changes. The Federal Reserve Board raises discount rates when it wants to check inflationary tendencies, lowers them when it wants to check deflationary tendencies. The Texas Railroad Commission lowers oil proration quotas when the demand and storage picture is unfavorable and raises quotas when these factors are favorable. The Federal

[13] See for an example of the problems Richard A. Tybout, *Government Contracting in Atomic Energy* (Ann Arbor, Mich., and London, England, 1956).

Communications Commission holds back television until it thinks it is sufficiently perfected, then begins to issue TV broadcasting licenses. A city traffic department experiments with the designation of one-way streets. The President raises the tariff rates on a commodity when he sees a threat to an industry needed in the defense effort, and his Administration adopts a policy of keeping oil imports down without imposing an order to that effect. As I prepare this copy I see in a weekly news journal that the government has moved on several fronts to give a bit more encouragement to home building:

1. FHA shaved from 7 to 5 per cent the down-payment on homes appraised at $9,000 or less.
2. The Federal Home Loan Bank Board boosted the amount that savings and loan associations can borrow to make mortgage loans.
3. The Federal National Mortgage Association liberalized certain of its policies.[14]

Shortly, other moves may be made in the same or the opposite direction.

This is not exactly what Holmes called the "fruitful empiricism" of the judicial process, in which men make a decision for a particular case and it becomes a precedent for other cases. This is judgment on a broader scale and for this time only. It is pragmatic in the fullest sense: there is no necessary aim of permanence; it is merely today's practical decision in the light of social ends which are accepted. It is government by men having continuous discretion. It is quality of government in a society of rapidly forging new development;

[14] *Newsweek,* October 1, 1956, p. 63.

it is characteristic of administration because it *only* can move promptly with new responses.

Men in government do, of course, seek ways of narrowing discretion. Such effort may be applauded if the limitations on results are recognized. The Federal Power Commission took a long step forward when it announced a policy for rate-making, the actual cost basis. This simplified many problems for the Commission and the industry, and gave a predictability to the process of rate-making which had not existed previously. Nevertheless, the Federal Power Commission refused to apply the policy all the way in the Hope case. The practical end declared by the Court in that case of balancing the interests of investors and consumers may not always be served by a single method. The ultimate act of discretion is often in the decision whether to follow or not to follow an existing standard.

Congress has sometimes laid down guides which were definite but proved unworkable or inadequate in practice. Familiar examples are the effort of 1920 to establish detailed guides for regulation of railroads and that of 1916 to make the fixing of tariff rates a mathematical process. More commonly Congress provides multiple, sometimes conflicting, standards to guide administrative agencies in policy development. Inevitably, discretion for administrators, albeit checked in many ways, has become a notable feature of administration.

V

The rule of law, like the maxim of efficiency, is an important goal for administration and an essential test of it. The rule of law manifests itself in so many ways that its full impact upon administration is great indeed. Yet discretion remains a significant attribute of administration at its higher levels. The rule of law, again, like the maxim of efficiency, becomes inadequate as a full measure of and guide for administration, primarily because of the importance of policy-making functions. If all administration were like that of the old age and survivors' insurance program, where men's rights are set forth in detail and administration is largely operations, then efficiency and the rule of law would be adequate tests and guides. Since administration has responsibility for policy making and program development, we must seek still other ideals which may govern its practice.

3

Administration by Competent and Responsible Men

IN 1940 PROFESSOR FRIEDRICH set forth a "dual tandard of administrative responsibility." Regarding olicy administratively formed he declared: ". . . we have right to call such a policy irresponsible if it can be hown that it was adopted without proper regard to the xisting sum of human knowledge concerning the tech- ical issues involved; we also have a right to call it rresponsible if it can be shown that it was adopted with- ut proper regard for existing preferences in the commu- ity, and more particularly its prevailing majority. Con- equently, the responsible administrator is one who is esponsive to these two dominant factors: technical nowledge and popular sentiment." Friedrich added hat the first standard could be called "objective," technical," or "functional" responsibility, and was a ype of responsibility of the "permanent administrator" alled upon to find "creative solutions for our crying echnical needs." The second standard was "political" esponsibility. To Friedrich political responsibility had een, even in Great Britain, "a noble goal rather than n actual achievement," and functional responsibility was "the new imperative."[1] Professor Finer pointedly objected on what he called "the cardinal issue of democratic government." He feared Professor Friedrich's views on functional responsibility led toward a new despotism of administrative government and objected to identification of political responsibility with responsiveness to "popular sentiment," rather than with responsibility to the representatives of the people. He believed that these should determine "the course of action of the public servants to the most minute degree that is technically feasible," and that the "various drawbacks of political control can be remedied."[2]

Thus, two eminent political scientists have from different European backgrounds restated for this country three answers on responsibility of administrators: adherence to technical or professional standards, responsibility to the people's representatives, and responsiveness to the community through all the ways in which its sentiments may be reflected. The last two of these relate to the ideal of democratic administration and are discussed in the next chapter. The first is the subject of this chapter.

Adherence to technical or professional standards is a result of competence and attitude. It means "the conduct of affairs by skilled persons" with professional

1 C. J. Friedrich and Edward S. Mason, *Public Policy, 1940* (Cambridge, Mass., 1940), pp. 8, 12-14.

2 Herman Finer, "Administrative Responsibility in Democratic Government," *Public Administration Review,* I (Summer, 1941), 335-50 For earlier statements by Friedrich and Finer, see Friedrich, "Responsible Government under the American Constitution," in Commission of Inquiry on Public Service Personnel, *Problems of the American Public Service* (New York, 1935), pp. 3-74, and Finer, "Better Government Personnel," *Political Science Quarterly,* LI (December, 1936), 580-85.

spirit.[3] It means administration by competent and responsible men.

We have sought in this country, as men have elsewhere, to attain this objective by developing a skilled bureaucracy. To state it differently, we have sought the attainment of the ideal of competence and responsibility by professionalization of the public service. This means of search for ideal will, therefore, be the subject of our comments.

Though a great advocate of constitutional government Woodrow Wilson declared in 1908: "Constitute them how you will, governments are always governments of men, and no part of any government is better than the men to whom that part is entrusted."[4] "It is the horse, not the harness, that draws the chariot," said Canning in 1801. This large truth that the quality of government is dependent upon the quality of men is far more pertinent today than when Canning or Wilson spoke. For all its great divisions, including administration, one ideal of man is that his government shall be conducted by competent and responsible men.

II

The requirements for toilers in the administrative vineyard are fixed by certain characteristics of their work. In administration responsibilities are divided and

[3] John Stuart Mill, from whom the quoted words on competence were taken, regarded reconciliation of the function of the expert and overhead control by the representatives of the people as *the* problem of government. See *Representative Government* (Everyman's ed. of *Utilitarianism, Liberty, and Representative Government,* New York, 1910), particularly pp. 247, 317.

[4] Woodrow Wilson, *Constitutional Government in the United States* (1908), p. 17.

allocated to units of organization, and within these to individuals. The allocations are made on the basis of some idea of function to be performed. The function may be one of process, such as recruiting personnel or purchasing supplies, or it may be one of primary purpose, such as constructing roads or protecting public health. In either case functional allocation is the first feature of administration. Adam Smith's principle of the division of labor, which for the economy and for the society as a whole is a natural development, is for administration a matter of design. Administration is, purposely, a functionally-organized instrument for a functionally-structured society.

As a result, specialization is the first characteristic of the administrator's task. He works in a unit of organization which has a specialized responsibility, and he works at a task which is specialized.

Increasingly, the tasks and problems in each specialized area have technical aspects. To grasp these technical aspects, differentiated or specialized knowledge is essential. This differentiated knowledge may be relatively simple in nature and readily obtainable by experience or training. In this day, however, the specialized knowledge and skill required for effective performance above the lowest levels in administration is acquired only by protracted periods of study or experience.

For wise judgment in a complex decisional situation several types of differentiated knowledge may need to be tapped and brought to bear on the problem being considered. For a single decision, inquiry into engineering or other scientific data, judgment on economic effects, analysis of legal angles, and appraisal of operating problems may be required.

For our society then, and for public administration in particular, it is necessary to recognize the basic facts of functional allocation and technical qualification. Long ago the courts arose as a functionally-differentiated structure and soon began to claim that the application, and the discovery, definition, or making of law in case-to-case proceedings was a technical task performable only by persons with a differentiated and esoteric body of knowledge and technique. What happened for this one area has been happening for other areas. Whether it be for forests, land use, road construction, banking, education or atomic energy, functional allocation and technical qualification are characteristic.

Yet I think we must make some distinctions regarding technicality and functionalism in administration. There are areas of administration where decision or action is dictated entirely, or almost entirely, by technical considerations. Examples are found in the work of the Bureau of Standards and the Patent Office. But functional responsibility, though used interchangeably with technical responsibility by Friedrich in his general discussion, may be broader than technical responsibility. There may be technical and non-technical aspects in a functional assignment. Particularly is this true where the functional allocation is not to an individual but to an organization and is for program rather than process. In this event functional responsibility may call for the co-ordination of several specialties and is itself not merely technical. Beyond this, there is interfunctional responsibility when the activities and decisions of two or more functional organizations interact or impinge on each other.

As one moves up the ladder from purely technical to larger spans of functional and interfunctional responsibility, expertness is still needed but the kind of expertness changes. It becomes the expertness of the generalist.

The function of the generalists has been variously defined. The Commission of Inquiry on Public Service Personnel saw need of an administrative group, comprehending the personnel involved in "general management, including such matters as organizing, staffing, directing, coordinating, planning, budgeting, and reporting."[5] Leonard White called it "general administration" and included co-ordination and policy formation. "General administration is understood to mean those duties concerned with the formation of policy, with the coordination and improvement of government machinery, and with the general management and control of the departments of the public service."[6] Donald Stone stressed the synthesizing aspect of top administration. "It requires competence in synthesizing and applying many disciplines in carrying out public purposes, and in the mobilization and use of a vast array of skills and techniques to achieve these purposes. It calls for sensitiveness to public relations, responsiveness, considerateness, a sense of the feasible."[7]

5 *Better Government Personnel: Report of the Commission of Inquiry on Public Service Personnel* (New York and London, 1935), p. 26.

6 Leonard D. White, *Introduction to the Study of Public Administration*, 3rd ed. (New York, 1948), p. 344.

7 Donald C. Stone, "The Top Manager and His Environment," in

Though these definitions complement each other to provide a comprehensive notion of the generalist function, Stone has in particular, in my opinion, keynoted its distinctive purpose in administration. It is a synthesizing expertness. It is expertness in correlation, balance, and choice. This synthesizing function involves grasp of the import upon policy of the diverse types of knowledge supplied by the technical experts on what is best and what is possible, and choice of the feasible in terms of workability, legal directives, and public acceptance. It involves selection and correlation among technical and nontechnical, factual and value, organic and human considerations. As I have said elsewhere, "The highest level of expertness is the point where synthesis is reached as a result of juncture of analysis of the obstinacies and flexibilities of organic factors with analysis of the obstinacies and amenabilities of people. This gets close to or includes the expertness of the statesman, whether administrative or political."[8]

The public service needs, therefore, a range of competences—from the technical to the interfunctional, from that of the pure specialist to that of the broad generalist.

III

It has now been 77 years since two events in 1881—the organization of the National Civil Service Reform League and the assassination of Garfield by a disap-

---

The Public Service and University Education, ed. Joseph E. McLean (Princeton, 1949), p. 65.

8 Emmette S. Redford, "The Protection of the Public Interest with Special Reference to Administrative Regulation," *American Political Science Review,* XLVIII (December, 1954), 1109.

pointed officeseeker—crystallized the drive for improvement in the quality and integrity of the public service. For a full half century the American public service had been characterized by amateurishness, brought about by the patronage system and the attendant lack of a career principle. The old system had been glorified by its champions as corollary of democracy, for it prevented office holding from being a right and office holders from being a class distinct from the populace. Lofty justification could not, however, becloud the corruption of politics and the inefficiency of administration. The new system rested upon the assumption that bureaucracy may be a correlative of, rather than an enemy of democracy. Its historical significance has been two-sided: it has been a means of changing the tone and purpose of politics, and it has been a response to the twin facts of functionalism and technicality in administration.

The trend of the efforts in recent years has been toward the professionalization of the public service. Professionalization as an ideal encompasses three things: first, qualifications for differentiated responsibilities; second, career opportunities for persons possessing requisite qualifications; and third, loyalty to the technical and ethical standards for differentiated occupational pursuits. As thus defined, professionalization is the means of attaining the objective of performance of public services by competent and responsible men.

The establishment of qualifications was at first associated with the idea of preventing political appointments. Similarly, the first step toward a career service was the prohibition of removal for political reasons.

It is unfortunate that the efforts to obtain an abl

and responsible public service were so long retarded by such a limited objective. It was, and is, however, the very first bastion to be conquered. There are still large areas in our state and local service where patronage produces amateurishness. The patronage system is, of course, heavily supported by the long ballot in state and local elections, and endures easily for types of employees who perform tasks on a low level of technicality. Nevertheless, great advances have been made toward the establishment of the principle of a nonpolitical bureaucracy. Tremendous steps were taken when the amendment of the Social Security Act required state and local employees working in programs established by that act to be under the merit system and when the Ramspeck Act brought most uncovered national employees under the civil service. And a major milestone was passed when a new Republican Administration, after twenty years of patronage poverty, moved into office with relatively minor compromises of the position of the permanent employee. At long last, the principles of nonpolitical appointment and nonremoval of those who have a fair claim on permanence of tenure have been firmly established at the national level. Impediment number one to the ideal of a competent and responsible public service still remains to be fought to the finish at other levels of our government.

For a generation now, and for longer in some of our cities, great efforts have been made toward enlarged objectives in government personnel programs. Dating from the reports of the Commission of Inquiry on Public Service Personnel in 1935 and of the Brownlow Committee in 1937, the new pitch became the positive one of creating a true career service so that competence and high morale could exist in the government service. Since that time progress has been made along the whole front of formal personnel methods—from recruitment to promotion. Attention has been concentrated, among other things, on training, responsibility of line officers, and service rather than control from the specialized personnel organizations. Continuously and from a multitude of directions the effort to get higher competence has proceeded.

Informed people now realize that there are large reservoirs of talent and experience on almost every subject in the public service. They have become accustomed to expecting an "informed judgment" from administrative agencies.

Nevertheless, there have been serious hindrances to an able public service. At the national level there have been four major obstacles to recruitment and retention of able men. First, the gap between the rewards in private and in public employment is large, and leadership has not presented to the public the serious nature of this problem. Large increases in salary at the higher levels are necessary to attract young men of talent to government service and limit the exodus of men from top-government to business positions. There has been much progress in developing legal safeguards for tenure; but this emphasis, if unaccompanied by a similarly strong emphasis on good remuneration, can itself contribute to mediocrity. Cost-of-living increases and the upgrading of positions at the end of the war have been palliatives but not an adequate solution at the upper levels. A second obstacle was the postwar conclusion of many who had gone through depression and wartime experiences that there was no longer the same stimulus from political leaders for imaginative and aggressive public service. One essential for retention of imaginative men is stimulating political leadership. Yet this is subject to tides of circumstance and popular sentiment and remains one of the silent ways the public gives or withholds stimulation of the public service to new adventures. Third, there was, in the words of Frederick M. Davenport, "the widespread and devastating and despairing—and often ignorant—criticism of the personnel and effectiveness of public servants."[9] That there was, as Herbert Emmerich has called it, "Scandal in Utopia" for a brief time did not justify the critical attitudes toward the public service and the undiscriminating attacks upon it. Finally, there were the excesses in the loyalty and security programs. The latter two situations brought to the public service, first loss of pride, and then fear. Moreover, youth shied away from entry into a service surrounded by suspicion and distrust. College students apparently agreed with William Penn, "A private Life is to be Preferr'd; the Honour and Gain of publick Posts, bearing no proportion with the Comfort of it."[10]

Happily, there is now more moderation and due process in security investigations and proceedings and

9 Frederick M. Davenport, "The Federal Service and Public Esteem," *Personnel Administration,* X, No. 4 (March, 1948), 1.

10 Quoted in *Public Administration Review,* XIII (Spring, 1953), 119, from William Penn, *Some Fruits of Solitude,* printed as an appendix, William Penn Tercentenary Committee, *Remember William Penn, 1644-1944* (Commonwealth of Pennsylvania, Department of Public Instruction, Pennsylvania Historical Commission, 1944).

less attack upon government servants, but it may take a generation and some bipartisan effort to overcome the attitudes developed in recent years toward a career in the public service.

Professionalization is, as we have seen, more than competence; it is also an attitude of mind toward one's work. It is loyalty to high professional standards in work performance. It is a quality of mind which finds honor and integrity in doing a job according to the ideals of a professional group.

All men have a kind of instinct of workmanship, as Veblen called it.[11] "Breathes there a man with soul so dead" that he is not motivated to do his daily work well? This desire is reinforced in the person who realizes that he has technical competence. The mechanic learns "the smell of burning oil from a hot bearing, the sight of reciprocating parts battering themselves to pieces through lack of proper timing, the acrid taste of spilled battery fluid, the uneven and irregular feel of vibration caused by faulty firing, the sound of chipped gear, with their infinite permutations and manifestations. . . ."[12] When he has acquired all this, response is intuitive, action is rational. It will be expert, it will be responsible. To make it otherwise would first require destruction of a man's soul.

Institutional factors may lend support to this natural impulse of man. First, membership in professional as-

[11] Friedrich has written a helpful chapter on "Responsibility and the Sense of Workmanship," Chapter VI of his *The New Belief in the Common Man* (Boston, 1943).

[12] A Government Employee, "Apologia Pro Vita Sua," *Public Administration Review,* X (Winter, 1950), 39.

sociations gives a sense of identity with others in the same occupational pursuit and strengthens the loyalty to professional standards. These standards become not only technical standards but group standards, and a desire for group approval supplements desire for technical validity. Second, internal devices may strengthen loyalty to professional standards. One of these, for example, is the arrangement sometimes made to allow the professional employee to file a statement of objection to action taken. This enables him to contribute from his competence to the pool of information and policy considerations but to retain his professional conscience. A different type of technique is delegation of authority to professional employees. The outstanding example is the delegation to examiners under the Administrative Procedure Act. Undoubtedly this has led to a sense of unity among these legal officers and to greater pride in their work. This device of delegation may be carried too far by including work involving group collaboration or mixture of policy application and policy determination, but it has great merit for pure application of legal or other technical standards. Finally, codes of conduct for professional groups may crystallize technical and ethical standards. The codes may be for a professional group in public and private employment, or for those members of the profession in public employment only. The Douglas Subcommittee on ethical standards in government suggested that professional groups consider adopting both types.[13] The best-known example

[13] *Ethical Standards in Government,* Report of a Subcommittee of the Committee on Labor and Public Welfare, U.S. Senate, 82nd Cong., 1st Sess., 1951, pp. 5, 35-36.

of a code for public officials is the long-existing code for city managers, which states standards in terms of the peculiarly public responsibilities of this group.

One task for the present is to move toward definition of professional ideals for the public service as a whole. Some agencies of the national government have drawn up codes for their employees, and at least one state has a legally-established code of conduct for public employees. Philip Monypenny has said that the enunciation of codes would give "the blessing of legitimacy" to standards of conduct, and that if sanctions were established to enforce the standards the individual employee would be "in a very different position from the individual faced with the pain of departure from his own personal standards."[14] The codes could include standards of ethical conduct and also standards of good administrative practice. They could perhaps go a long way toward inculcating a common sense of professional purpose among government employees.

We can all agree I think with John Gaus' conclusion: "Certainly, in the system of government which is now emerging, one important kind of responsibility will be that which the individual civil servant recognizes as due to the standards and ideals of his profession. This is 'his inner check'."[15] But we may not all agree with the statement in the 1936 *Municipal Yearbook* "that self-control by professional groups of the officials themselves

[14] Philip Monypenny, "A Code of Ethics as a Means of Controlling Administrative Conduct," *Public Administration Review,* XIII (Summer, 1953), 187.

[15] John M. Gaus, "The Responsibility of Public Administration," in Gaus, Leonard D. White, and Marshall E. Dimock, *The Frontiers of Public Administration* (Chicago, 1936), p. 40.

is the key opening the door to effective democracy."[16] Friedrich saw that the problem of democracy raised another issue. John Gaus saw still another problem when he said that "official recognition" could be given to "the responsibility of the civil servant to the standards of his profession, *insofar as those* standards make for the public interest. . . ."[17] These ideals of democracy and public interest reach beyond, indeed may qualify, the ideal of professionalization.

IV

Set against the advantages of professionalization in administration are the hazards of government by bureaucracy. I think these are inertness, separation, and specialization. Each will be discussed briefly.

Listing of inertness as one of three dangers of bureaucracy will come as a surprise to some. We have been told by some that bureaucrats are overly aggressive, that they constantly want to expand their activities, that they supply the initiative on which legislation is based. All of these things may at times be true, but the more likely possibility is that bureaucracies will in time become sluggish, self-satisfied, and interested in the survival of their existing habits and thought patterns.

It can be expected that domestic society and international power relations will change with enough speed that adaptation will be needed constantly in government policies and that this adaptation will require creative imagination at many thinking centers. We must hope that professionals in a hierarchy will make many new

16 At p. 211.
17 Gaus, White, and Dimock, p. 39. (My italics.)

discoveries or initiate many changes in policy; yet we should be conscious also of the danger that their responsiveness to new conditions and new public needs may be limited by the habits of large, complex, going organizations. An organization evolves its course of action and its thought patterns, and when these have been set it may take strong impetus from above and outside to bring adaptation to new conditions. Even the various parts of organizations often develop their own ways of thought and their own vested interests. The individual bureaucrat learns that initiative is often disturbing and suspect, that there are many obstacles to change from an existing pattern, and that long-delayed adaptations can be made only with push from the top. It is easier, therefore, for him to be resigned than to be aggressive.

The second danger of bureaucracy is that it will be separated in attitude and purpose from the surrounding society. It may, because of professionalism, class orientation, over-centralization, or a natural inwardness, lose contact with opinion, particularly lay opinion, outside the organization.

Consciousness of this danger was part of the reason for American fears of bureaucracy in the nineteenth century. It has also been a reason for the reluctance of Americans to consider the adoption of a closed upper division in the administrative service, such as Great Britain has.

Norton Long has argued that the American civil service is democratic in composition:

The democratic character of the civil service stems from its origin, income level, and associations. The process of selection of the civil service, its contacts, milieu, and income level after induction make the civil service as a body a better sample of the mass of the people than Congress.[18]

Undoubtedly methods of recruitment and the general fluidity, rather than rigid bureaucratization, of the American public service have kept it from developing a class character. On the other hand, its connections at the Washington level are to a large extent intraservice and clientele, and the Congress—because of its renewability and approachableness—will probably be a better reflection of the tides of popular opinion. Long's major point is a strong one: the pluralism of the community can be reflected only in pluralism within the government. The bureaucracy, if kept open and fluid, can supplement the political branches in representation of the people. On the other hand, it is obvious that bureaucracy needs constant supplementation. Any one who has served in a bureaucratic organization knows the ever-present tendency toward inwardness, and even the danger of development of distrust and fear, if not disdain, of lay opinion.

The most persistent cause of separateness and the greatest danger of bureaucracy arises from its specialization. As Wallace Sayre has said, specialization "is one of our greatest national strengths—but it has its costs." He notes three types of costs: (1) the specialist is not disposed to take a balanced view; (2) specialization creates administrative difficulties "of coordination, unity, and coherence"; (3) "one of the tendencies of specialization is to maximize the objective facts and characteristics of

18 Norton E. Long, "Bureaucracy and Constitutionalism," *American Political Science Review,* XLVI (September, 1952), 808-18. Quotation from p. 813.

a problem and to minimize its acceptance, the understanding of it and the consensus about it which prevails in the general society."[19]

It is generally agreed that the American public service has been overspecialized. Job definitions have been overrefined and types of education and experience overlimited. This has created difficulties in transfer of personnel and in selection of persons for higher positions. Nevertheless, the need for specialization cannot be escaped. Rowland Egger has reminded us that fully 85 per cent of the positions both in Great Britain and in this country are specialized.[20]

The problems of individual specialization are magnified by the necessary organizational specialization. Each functional organization develops its own self-centered attitudes. For protection it reaches to groups and organizations with similar purpose. Bureaus of government cultivate ties with committee members and staffs which work in the same problem areas. They also establish close affiliations with clientele groups outside the government who have a parallel interest in the program objectives of the agency. Arthur Maass has vividly described for us the close ties between the Army Engineers, the committees of Congress, and lobbying groups such as the National Rivers and Harbors Congress—ties which have produced rule, as James Rowe has said, "by a triumvirate, by a clique, by a bureau-clientele-com-

19 Wallace S. Sayre, "The Public Service—Its Future Status," in *Democracy in Federal Administration*, ed. O. B. Conoway, Jr. (Graduate School, U.S. Department of Agriculture, Washington, 1956), p. 68.

20 In a chapter in McLean, *Public Service*, pp. 211-14.

mittee chairman form of government."[21] In education, health, or other activities similar though less institutionalized affiliations could be found. James M. Beck once said that Congress could not "cope with the combined interests of these private associations and the bureaucracy,"[22] but he did not anticipate the key problem of a society of parallel functionalism, where liaison would exist between administrative and congressional bureaucracies, congressional committee members, and private groups.

Professionalization, as York Willbern has so vividly shown, can contribute to this functional separatism. Regarding the professions he says: "Forming, as they frequently do, an impeccably correct and proper link between governmental personnel and groups wanting or needing something from government (as all groups do), they present a type of *built-in* representation of a special type of special interest." He further states that the desire of the professional groups for independence of the functions with which they are associated "shatters general political control."[23]

21 James H. Rowe, Jr., *American Political Science Review,* XLVI (June, 1952), 572, reviewing the thorough analysis of the subject in Arthur Maass, *Muddy Waters: The Army Engineers and the Nation's Rivers* (Cambridge, Mass., 1951). For briefer treatment see Maass' article, "Congress and Water Resources," *American Political Science Review,* XLIV (September, 1950), 576-93.

22 James M. Beck, *Our Wonderland of Bureaucracy* (New York, 1932), p. 92.

23 York Y. Willbern, "Professionalization in the Public Service: Too Little or Too Much?" *Public Administration Review,* XIV (Winter, 1954), 15, 16. (His italics.)

V

The service to society of functional and technical expertness must be magnified and at the same time means be found to minimize the dangers inherent in a professionalized bureaucracy. To a large extent the latter objective must be attained by political controls—to be discussed in the next chapter. But it is possible also that the complementary objectives may be attained, in part, within the bureaucracy itself.

One way of attacking this problem is through efforts to keep the public service flexible. This may be done through a variety of approaches. The first is to keep the public service open at every level to entry by persons from outside. The open civil service is a qualification of the career principle, for it limits the opportunities for advancement from the lower levels of the career service. This qualification will not, however, be serious if preference, other things equal, is given to the career employee who possesses equal qualifications, and if the number of those entering from the outside is not large. Actually, the number is not likely to be significant unless effort is made to make it such. The normal avenue of refreshment of the public service from the outside will be adoption of new programs or shifts in the requirements of old programs which call for new types of personnel or for a larger number of employees. And up to now the expansion of government has presented more of a problem of assimilation of outsiders than of fertilization of the public service by their entry.

The opportunities for an open civil service will vary with the type of service. It is not practicable for specialties where there is no comparable professional service outside, as in military planning and operations. But even in the military service there are opportunities for infusion of outside, civilian personnel, as in logistics, budgeting, and personnel, and the very existence of a tight career service for the purely military phases is argument for continuous infusion of personnel into the military services from other public services or from business or other private pursuits. For most process specialties of the auxiliary or staff type, such as legal service, accounting and budgeting, personnel administration, and economic research, there are potentialities for outside recruitment. The same is true of many, perhaps most, substantive specialties, such as those in health, welfare, and highway construction.

Yet the possibilities of infusing highly qualified personnel into the upper levels of the public service from outside are not great. The reason is the differential between salaries in public and private employment. Because of this differential other means for attaining the end desired are likely to be more fruitful, and less disturbing to the public service. One of these is the use of consultants and temporary employees. There are dangers in recruitment of these from clienteles closely affected by an agency's programs—the danger that they will have two masters whose interests are in conflict. But these dangers can in large measure be avoided by discretion in the choice and use of consultants and temporary employees.

The more hopeful procedures are those looking toward flexibility within the public service itself. Notable are the developments in training. The granting of fellowships for study at the Littauer Center, the assignment of military personnel to civilian colleges for new training, the tremendous growth of facilities for study at the graduate schools in the Department of Agriculture and the universities in the Washington area illustrate a trend which should receive further emphasis. Similar is the occasional use of outside experts in in-service training sessions. These arrangements are likely to be particularly advantageous if they throw the public servant into contact with new and wider fields of knowledge, which though they may appear to be peripheral nevertheless serve to acquaint him with the new developments which are occurring within society. Other arrangements which should be mentioned are those for transfer within the public service. Notable are the rules for rotation of home service and foreign service personnel in the Department of State, and efforts to arrange for transfers between Washington and field stations within this country. Similarly advantageous would be flexible arrangements for interchange of personnel between state and local service on the one hand and the federal service on the other. All such developments accord with the career principle and the idea of a professionalized public service, but at the same time keep it attuned to the society in which it functions.

Another means of overcoming the hazards of bureaucracy is through a layer of generalists at the top level of the professional service. There would be two potential advantages in the existence of such a layer. First, it would provide protection for the specialist. The professional working as a specialist should be a purist, whether he be teacher, accountant, physician, or scientist. To be less would be to sell his soul and fail in his obligation to society. If there are compromises to be made because of limitation of funds or political or interest pressure, these should be determined on another plane of operation. Compromise cannot be mixed with the specialist task without overextending the function of politics and undermining the service of technical analysis. In government as elsewhere a ring of protection should be run around the specialist so that his function *qua* specialist may be performed with fidelity to his trust.

In his thoughtful book on *Government and Science* Don Price sees the dangers that scientists may try "to assume responsibilities semipolitical in nature" and politicians try to interfere with the conditions of scientific research. He proposes "an intervening layer of administration between science and politics, to protect science and to make their relationship more smooth."[24] When the present president of my university was inaugurated, my colleague Professor Walter P. Webb, speaking for the faculty, turned to the incoming president and reminded him that the faculty would expect him to stand on the battlements and protect their freedoms. In effect, Price and Webb were both saying that guardianship of the integrity of the functional specialist against the political overhead is one aspect of the responsibility of the top bureaucracy.

The second potential benefit of an intermediate level of generalists is that they may supply the breadth of view, the appreciation of the interrelatedness of functional specialties, the understanding of the necessity

[24] Don K. Price, *Government and Science: Their Dynamic Relation in American Democracy* (New York, 1954), pp. 202, 108-09.

for correlation of technical data and political purpose which produces the true synthesizing expert so sorely needed in this pluralistic society. The Task Force on Personnel and Civil Service of the Second Hoover Commission had in mind this potential benefit when in appraising the functions of an intermediate layer, to be called the senior civil service, it listed among its utilities both emphasis on "matters of feasibility, practicality, and effectiveness" and ability "to seek the balance of interests which is the continuous function of government."[25]

For over twenty years now there has been argument for structuring and professionalizing the generalist function. The Commission of Inquiry on Public Service Personnel first gave impetus to the idea when it differentiated the work of the "administrative service."[26] The idea persists in one way or another. It may be seen in the earlier development of our first professionalized generalists in the public service—the city managers—and in the recent development of the manager function in the mayor-manager system in some of our largest cities. It may be seen also in the unification of top managerial functions in the governor's office in some states and in departmental offices of the national service, and in the emergence of general staff functions at departmental and presidential levels. It appears again in the aforementioned recommendation of the Task Force for a senior civil service.

The Task Force desired a flexible group of top level administrators "with a substantial area of transferabil-

25 *Task Force Report on Personnel and Civil Service* (Washington, 1955), pp. 3-4.

26 *Better Government Personnel,* pp. 32-36.

ity." These would serve as administrative assistant secretaries in departments, heads and members of departmental management offices, deputy heads and other members of departmental staff offices concerned with substantive policy, and chiefs of "line (or operating) bureaus." There would be about 1500 of these top level administrators in the senior civil service.

There has been much disagreement over details of the proposal for a senior civil service. In my opinion the basic idea of professionalization of the generalist function in the civil service is a good one. It is a means of enlarging competence at the apex, where functional and interfunctional synthesis are so urgently needed as complement to technical competence existing at the lower ranges of the bureaucracy. Yet it will probably be worked on in less distinct ways than visualized in the proposal of the Task Force. First, I doubt whether the line between the political officers and the top civil servants can be drawn as simply organizationally or as rigidly functionally as the Task Force proposes. Some bureaus are now and undoubtedly should be headed by permanent civil servants; for others it may be the legitimate view of a new administration that they cannot be made responsive without change in their headship. As for function, there is a thin line, to say the least, between the administrative statesmanship which comprehends the forces of society as well as technical feasibilities and the political statesmanship which comprehends feasibilities as well as political motivation. Second, it may be regarded as desirable to allow freedom of entry from many avenues into the senior service. The proposal of the Task Force to require five years experience in federal service for entry into the senior civil service would prevent the refreshing of the upper ranks from state and municipal service, business administration, or other pursuits. Movement out of the senior service into political positions with freedom to return might also be desirable. The top civil service may be a needed source for political appointments, and the possibility of a return to the civil service would facilitate this recruitment. Third, it may be that all that can be done is to establish categories within which transferability would be attempted. There is much difference, for example, between the nature of work in management services and controls and that in economic and social analysis and planning; it may be that a complete generalist will be a rare bird and that the generalist group itself will always have some dividing lines, though perhaps not so rigid as to prevent their occasional crossing.

Finally, as Wallace Sayre has pointed out, there are additional ways of developing expertness in general administration.[27] One is to recruit "a larger supply of young generalists." These could be given a variety of assignments in their early years in the service. A second is an executive development program, such as was recommended by the Task Force and through which men with competence for general administration would be spotted and given training and experience toward that end. A third would be a program designed to infuse broader perspectives into the thinking of the specialists who are rising toward top administrative positions in the national service. For, as Don Price says, "the only

[27] Sayre, pp. 68-69.

hope for an adequate administrative corps in the American government is to build it in part on the generalist with a background in general management and general public affairs, and in part on the man who has become a generalist after a thorough grounding in one of the specialized sciences or in its engineering or managerial application.[28]

VI

Service by competent and responsible men is one of the great ideals for administration. Attainment of this ideal in our complex society requires professionalization of the public service. Professionalization, in turn, brings problems. These problems can be met in part by policies designed to keep the public service flexible and fluid within and open to some measure of fertilization from outside. They can be further met by developing within the public service a full range of competences—from the technical and functional to the superfunctional, from the specialist to the generalist. These things will not, however, fully solve the problems of inertia, separatism, and specialization within the bureaucracy. For further solutions the last two answers of Friedrich and Finer to the problem of responsibility will have to be examined.

28 Price, p. 202.

4

Whence Democracy?

THIS CHAPTER is on the great ideal of democracy as related to the administrative function. Stated differently it deals with Professor Finer's objective that the administrator shall be responsible to the people's representatives and Professor Friedrich's objective that he shall be responsive to popular sentiment.

Some years ago Lord Hewart frightened many with his description of administrative powers as creating "the New Despotism." Later, James Burnham foretold the rise of a managerial class in business and government which would be a new oligarchy in society. Robert Michels wrote about the "iron law of oligarchy" as a tendency inhibiting democratic controls in all organizations. Hayek and Mises have also, though quite extravagantly, argued that the modern welfare state would place our liberties at the mercy of new bureaucracies.[1]

[1] Hewart of Bury, *The New Despotism* (New York, 1929; London, 1945); James Burnham, *The Managerial Revolution* (New York, 1941); Robert Michels, *Political Parties: A Sociological Study of the Oligarchical Tendencies of Modern Democracy,* trans. Eden and Cedar Paul (New York, 1915); F. A. Hayek, *The Road to Serfdom* (Chicago, 1944); Ludwig von Mises, *Omnipotent Government* (New Haven, 1944).

These categorizations and prophecies seem remote and unrealistic to most Americans, for their struggle has been to substitute professionalization for amateurishness and rotation in office, and they have never had reason to fear the grosser ills of bureaucratic government. Yet if the American fears less "in the gross," he is still concerned that administration in its refinements reflect the requirements of democratic government.

Usually this is discussed as a problem of "controls on behalf of the people." The term "controls" is adopted here and used broadly to include both check and supply. There must be check or counterpoise from the people and their representatives; but democracy serves a greater function when it *supplies* direction and spirit for the professional service.

Whence democracy? There are many views of democracy, and some of these are inacceptable or must be used with caution in a discussion of democratic control of the bureaucracy. One idea is that of "democracy within administration," which means participation of the employees of an organization in determining its actions. Employee participation may be valuable for morale or as a recognition of human dignity; it may be essential for rational decision making; but it is irrelevant to the problem of democratic control. Administrative agencies are not society; they are servants of society. Employee participation has no function in the enforcement of this servant position. Indeed, it may stand in conflict, for employee participation may qualify hierarchical direction. Sometimes integration and hierarchy are discussed as being in themselves anti-democratic because they have authoritarian implications with respect to workers in organization.[2] This confuses the position of the workers with that of the society which they are to serve. Democratic government assumes that administration must be subject to control from outside, and integration and hierarchy are devices for insuring this subjection all the way down the line.

Democracy has been defined also in terms of participation by affected groups outside administration. Discussing lay participation in administration Walter Gellhorn concluded: "affected private interests are shaping the course of official action. It is Democracy at work."[3] But I think Gellhorn was correct when he qualified this sweeping statement by recognizing that it was dangerous doctrine if not strictly limited in its applications. Consideration in appropriate ways of private interests affected by policy is administrative due process. But it would be democratic also only if the private interests which "shaped the course of official action" were the interests of the community, or if the area in which action was shaped included only technical feasibilities and tailoring of requirements within the confines of purpose determined by persons more nearly representative of the whole community. Group representation in some form may be an element of democracy in a pluralistic society but not if it is achieved by delegation of matters *of public concern* to groups inadequately representative

2 For an interesting exchange of opinion on this see Dwight Waldo, "Development of Theory of Democratic Administration," *American Political Science Review,* XLVI (March, 1952), 81-103, and Peter F. Drucker, "'Development of Theory of Democratic Administration': Replies and Comments," *ibid.,* (June, 1952), 496-500.

3 Walter Gellhorn, *Federal Administration Proceedings* (Baltimore, 1941), p. 130. (Gellhorn's capitalization.)

of the public. The ill-fated NRA (1933-35) illustrated the shaping of official action by private groups, but the arrangements for public representation were so poor that it could hardly be called an example of democratic administration.

Democracy, like public interest, is an inclusive concept. The concept is inseparable from that of people, public, or community. This does not mean that the community itself is not multiple diversity or can be represented in all its varieties by any single process. It does mean that government is not democratically responsible or responsive to "popular sentiment" unless the totality of its processes gives representation both to the unities and to the many varieties of the community.

What are the ways of achieving this ideal for administration? Whence democratic check and supply? I discussed in the last chapter one set of means—those which aim to insure that bureaucracy will not be a separate class. There are others which seek to insure that the people will have ample opportunities for access to administration or that administrators may know the desires of the people. Still others provide for participation of the public or portions thereof in the process of administration. And finally there are the relations of the administration to the elected representatives of the people.

II

We discuss first the direct contacts with the public rather than its representatives. Can there be check and supply for the bureaucracy through its public relations?

One possibility is lay participation, that is by persons

in the community who though they may acquire a kind of official position by taking an oath, nevertheless are unpaid, or virtually unpaid, part-time workers. In administration of national programs which have had to be carried to millions of people over this vast nation there has been considerable use of local lay participation. The system has been employed in administration of selective service, wartime rationing, and agricultural conservation and stabilization programs. In the first two the lay participation has been community participation, in the last it is participation only by interests directly affected. In each case a government which lacks, except for the post offices, going centers of administration in the communities, has been provided with a means of getting program in effect in every community.

Summarizing the advantages of community, volunteer participation in rationing I have written as follows:

> It provided a means of administration—a method of getting rations to the people promptly and with a minimum of inconvenience. It helped get public acceptance of the idea of rationing and the justice of individual decisions. It provided local participation in a national program. All, in all, it served to bridge the gap between the national plan and the folks who lived under it.

On the other hand, I concluded that "unevenness and laxity are to be expected when volunteers are used."[4]

Lay administration will usually be less efficient than bureaucratic administration. But, like the jury system, it is educator of people and safety valve for government. Though he stated the problem of government as recon-

[4] Emmette S. Redford, *Field Administration of Wartime Rationing* (Washington, 1947), p. 173. See also pp. 23-25.

ciliation of "the conduct of affairs by skilled persons" and control by representative bodies,[5] Mill yet emphasized how "salutary is the moral part of the instruction afforded by the participation of the private citizen, if even rarely, in public functions."[6] There is danger today that people who in small government might have felt that policy of government was a shared experience may regard themselves as only recipients of service and money or subjects of control. Citizen participation in meaningful ways may provide a sense of personal contribution and, using Mill's words again, an "unselfish sentiment of identification with the public."[7] But while community participation educates the community, it also educates the administrators on what is acceptable and moderates the tendency of administrators to live in a shell of rule and system. Lay administration has its limits and creates great problems of instruction and supervision, but it has value in attuning government to people.

Another means of lay participation is in the agricultural referendum. This may be a democratic device if the referendum is limited to choices which have meaning only for or primarily for farmers. It ceases, I believe to be a democratic device in any case where issues of policy seriously affecting the public are subject to determination by farmer ballot.

Lay participation has also been provided in the

[5] John Stuart Mill, *Representative Government* (Everyman's ed. of *Utilitarianism, Liberty, and Representative Government,* New York 1910), p. 247.

[6] *Ibid.,* p. 217.

[7] *Ibid.*

use of a part-time public board for direction of the administration of a program. This method of keeping administration responsive has rarely been employed in our national administration, but has been common in state and local administration, especially for such services as education, health, and welfare.

I wish we had more scholarly analysis of this device. It certainly has brought to administration the interest and ideas of outstanding community leaders, and conversely has had an educative effect upon these participants. At the same time, lay responsibility for top management and policy direction has its disadvantages. It strengthens functional independence and impedes co-ordination, and the argument against it is strong where continuing co-ordination with other functions is needed. It has been a device for keeping politics out of administration. Has it done so? Or has it channeled politics into hidden and irresponsible channels? Is it a device for political societies which have not developed the conditions for responsible party leadership? Or which have not yet developed insulation against politics in the standards of a professionalized public service? On the other hand, has it removed too much from politics? Has it kept questions out of the political channel which should have been considered there? Has it prevented discussion and education of the public on significant issues? Has it, in other words, interposed lay participation at so high and determinative a level as to limit seriously public representation to a few unaccountable members of the public?

How do lay boards obtain the information on which they operate? Must it not come to them from the bureaucracy they are to control? Without a study and planning staff of its own and without time for full-time analysis of problems, can a lay board provide the degree of democratic control over the bureaucracy that is needed? Is not the lay board a weak instrument of democracy for large, complex, or technical undertakings? Moreover, where there is a strong professional group interest in the work of an agency, is there not danger that the lay board will overrepresent such an interest and not provide a really independent control on behalf of the society as a whole?

This is one of the most troublesome issues in the organization of public authority. I venture the suggestion, however, that except for the professional licensing board, the lay board with determinative authority will not be widely adopted in new types of public service, at least in those jurisdictions where a professionalized public service and a two-party system exist.[8] On the other hand, extension of lay participation at the top level of administration through another means, namely the advisory committee, may be expected.

The type of advisory committee most common is one which represents clienteles specially affected by an agency's program. Such committees are channels through which administrators may obtain information on technical feasibilities and on the level of performance or legal requirement which will be accepted by affected groups. They also give an administrative agency opportunities to make its viewpoint known to group leaders and to obtain their concurrence and support. Yet they

[8] See pp. 94-96 for discussion of the working relations between bureaucracy and political officials.

carry the great danger that they will provide uneven access to administrative agencies and thus distort their programs toward those group interests which are strongly represented on the committees. This may arise because the committees are unrepresentative of the special clienteles they purport to represent. In large government there is always danger that access will be limited to the "large and near," and this danger can be accentuated by advisory committees. In the Office of Price Administration the regional offices complained that advisory committees were unrepresentative of industry groups. They finally succeeded in obtaining a concession that they would be given a part in selecting advisory committees. It was hoped that in that way the response of the agency to the problems of all types of business in all sections of the country could be improved. The danger of uneven access may arise also because the latent and unorganized interests of the community generally are not represented. The effect may be to accentuate any tendency which exists in the agency to overlook general interests and to pursue lines of policy which accord with the interests of clientele groups.

Some might argue, therefore, that consultation with advisory committees may be justified as due process for affected groups but that it is not a democratic device. But democracy is a complex and multifeatured process. Safeguards for responsive administration may rest in part in restrained use of some methods which if used without care and balanced judgment may defeat the purposes of the state. Certainly, the most obvious conclusion about advisory committees is that stated by Arthur Macmahon years ago that "only by careful use of advisory boards will the danger of compromising administration at its core be avoided."[9]

The dangers to be avoided are not so great where the advisory committee represents the interests of the community as a whole. A local library or hospital committee may reflect the composition of society's informed leadership. To the extent that it does, it is potentially a means of making administration responsive to the needs and desires of people but carries small danger of inhibiting overhead democracy.

A second way of insuring responsiveness is through decentralized operations and facilities. This can be done through use of governments of smaller territorial jurisdictions, as in local enforcement of state law, or state and local co-operation in carrying out national programs. Or it can be done by establishment of field offices by national or state governments. There are some common motivations for decentralization in either case. In part, they are the requirements for effective program administration and public convenience. Beyond this, they are the requirements for responsive government. Administration is not fully responsive if adjustments are not made to dissimilar conditions in different parts of a vast land. Nor is it responsive if access to it is not possible for all who may be affected. Local offices are necessary to give to people in general some facility in access, so as to equalize in some measure the greater opportunities for those who are "in the know" in Washington and state capitols and whose business justifies travel to distant centers. They are necessary to provide

[9] "Boards, Advisory," *Encyclopedia of the Social Sciences* (New York, 1930), I, 611.

the administrators sitting in distant offices with a flow of information on human reactions, so that they may know what their programs are doing for and to people. There is great danger that the tremendous advantages of local offices may be overlooked by top administrators.

A final way of insuring responsiveness is through the sampling of public opinion. Agencies often make arrangements for clipping the daily and weekly press, and they may supplement this—perhaps much more in the future—with polls on public reaction to their policies. They are likely to give particular attention to trends and opinions reflected in trade and professional publications. Administrators also attend professional meetings and meetings of clientele groups which they serve. All of this heightens the sensitivity of administration, and if the reach for opinion is wide enough the responsiveness of administration may be broadened.

There are two main types of fear or reservation about these various means of public participation and contact. The first is that the agencies will be provided with facilities through which they can control public response to their activities. In the midterm of OPA's life a former editor who was resigning from the agency referred to the agency's local boards and advisory committees and said, "This agency has built a propaganda machine which can control the thought of the American people." His fears proved to be unfounded, as was demonstrated by the subsequent curtailments of power and ultimate death sentence for the agency. Every means of contact is, indeed, a two-way street. Lay units of participation, local offices, and the press can be used as channels for obtaining public support for administration. But such support is a vital necessity for program effectiveness. Agencies must be allowed facilities for obtaining it if they are to accomplish anything for the public. So long as public support rests on understanding, and so long as there are means for uncovering false claims, the effort to obtain consensus is positive good rather than evil. Use of devices for public contact usually brings response at both ends of the street, and insures that the response of administration and public alike is based on more complete understanding of the position and needs of the other.

The other fear is that the public relations activities will not provide sufficiently wide public access to administration to be really democratic. The agencies are likely to develop close associations with those who have the largest immediate interest in their work. They may have little continuing contact with other segments of the public. In the establishment of the agency's program by the Congress the many needs or interests affected probably had, by virtue of the complexity of the legislative process and the diversities of representation therein, opportunities to present their needs. If administration is to be democratic a similarly broad opportunity for public access to it must be safeguarded.

The most significant limitation of these means of check and supply is that they can be interstitial only. They cannot provide the primary statement of governing purpose, financial resources, supplementation or curtailment of power through new legislation, or overhead co-ordination with other programs. These elements of supply and check can come only from the representative system.

III

The primary means of democratic control is through the representative system. This is overhead democracy, through which administration derives its existence, powers, and responsibilities. Without this overhead control administration would itself be the top political institution, which would be an impossible assumption. Administration is in essence a subordinate function, and its subordination in representative government is presumed to be to the supremacy of the representative organs. The position of the representative organs as trustees for the people and the derivative function of administration fix the first canon of administrative ethics. That canon is allegiance to the properly declared will of the representatives. Without this, government cannot be democracy as well as bureaucracy.

This need not mean, as Finer argued, that the representatives should "determine the course of action of the public servants to the most minute degree that is technically feasible."[10] Charles Hyneman seems to have more correctly stated the proper principle when he wrote, "And Congress should not define and describe a governmental undertaking in such detail that administrative officials are rendered incapable of achieving the major objectives toward which the legislation is directed."[11] The ideal of democracy does not mean that the representatives shall determine or even take note of all policy; it means rather that they shall be able to

[10] *Supra,* p. 50.

[11] Charles S. Hyneman, *Bureaucracy in a Democracy* (New York, 1950), p. 85.

set forth guide lines of purpose and to take corrective action if purpose is perverted in detailed elaboration and execution.

Nor is the claim for supremacy of representative institutions a simple claim for majority rule. There is usually no majority popular opinion on an issue before the representatives. If so, it is usually impossible to know whether their decision accords with the majority popular opinion. The decision may represent more than majority opinion because it is the concurrent will of House, Senate, and the President, and the will of each is a concurrency of many influences. Our system can be more representative than majority rule, party rule, or even concurrent majorities, for the very diversity of its elements may insure that the totality of expertness and the totality of pluralities and unities may be components of decision. Or it may be less representative than either majority rule, party rule, or concurrent majorities because it provides opportunities for unrepresentative pieces of the system to influence the administration of policy, and because its very complexity prevents ready access by administration to the representative system for new guides on policy.

The system provides representation both of the unity and the plurality of society. The presidency is, of course, the only formal representative of the unities of interest and ideal in the nation, but these unities are pushed into focus through the pressure of facts upon committees and members of Congress, the supraconstituency position achieved on some problems by leading Congressmen and Senators, and the process of distilling policy out of multiple claims. The diversities of a pluralistic society are reflected also, not only within the Congress, but within the administrative organization which underlays the presidency and in the pressures brought to bear on that office from the outer, popular constituency.

With all its imperfections the representative system composed of President and Congress is the clearest embodiment of the ideal of democracy, as it is also of the ideal of supremacy of law. Having fixed this anchor point, it is possible to state the first of four propositions of fact or principle on democratic control.

It is simply this: the President must have control of administration. This is traditional and modern principle: it accords with the intention of the Framers who made the President the head of the executive branch of the government, and it was affirmed strongly by the Report of the President's Committee on Administrative Management in 1937 and by the first Hoover Commission. It is a democratic principle for it declares the subordination of all administrative agents to a responsible representative of the people.

To safeguard his responsibility the President needs a sufficient and qualified corps of political executives. Their function, as stated by the Task Force on Personnel and Civil Service reporting to the Second Hoover Commission, is "to represent within the administration the policy purposes of the President, to bring the general public's point of view to bear upon administrative decisions, to provide leadership in developing policy, to exercise statutory powers vested in them as public officials, and to act for the Chief Executive in seeing that all of the laws are faithfully executed; in short, to take the responsibility for governing."[12] The political execu-

12 *Task Force Report on Personnel and Civil Service* (Washington, 1955), p. 1.

tives are the President's men; they represent him in positions from which they can direct and control, and take responsibility for, the activities of the career administrators.

The Task Force declared that "the role of this entire group of political party executives is at the heart of representative government."[13] The justification for the statement lies in the inability of Congress to provide continuing direction and control of the administration and in the position of the President as the representative of the nation.

The Eisenhower Administration helped clarify the need for political responsibility for administrative activity by setting up Schedule C, a separate category of noncareer public officials including primarily those having top policy-making functions. The Task Force built upon this idea and argued that "there should be an increase in the number of positions of political leadership and responsibility."[14] Whatever the number, it should be sufficient to provide opportunity for a new administration to put its policies, within the confines of statutory and constitutional limitations, into effect and to insure that the President can discharge his constitutional responsibility to see that the laws are faithfully executed. Paul Appleby has stated it briefly as the need for "sufficient political officers to enforce political responsibility."[15]

A more difficult problem than number is competence.

[13] *Ibid.*

[14] *Ibid.*, p. xiii.

[15] Paul H. Appleby, *Morality and Administration in Democratic Government* (Baton Rouge, La., 1952), p. 55.

The Task Force saw that at "the topmost level these men require both well-developed executive ability and well-developed qualities of political leadership," and that "at lower levels . . . they must have great capacity quickly to penetrate the mysteries of complex and technical operations, analytical ability of a high order, and a gift for working with people." It concluded that "the capacities which are so essential in political executives are nowhere systematically developed in American life. American society has not bred executives for political leadership."[16]

Each administration will face this problem in its own way. The Task Force on Personnel and Civil Service pointed out that roughly fifty per cent of the incumbents in pre-existing jobs placed in Schedule C were retained and, in addition, twenty per cent of all Schedule C positions were filled by promotion, reassignment or transfer of federal employees who were in the service prior to the change in administration.[17] The recruitment by a Republican Administration of seventy per cent of its political staff from persons who had been serving in a Democratic Administration re-emphasizes the importance of a broad-gauged career service and of opportunities for transferability from the administrative to the political service. It also shows the great difficulty of recruiting competent political executives from outside the executive hierarchy. The Eisenhower Administration drew heavily from business; another administration may draw more largely from state houses and city halls, which are breeding centers for political

16 *Report on Personnel and Civil Service,* p. 40.
17 *Ibid.,* p. 37.

executives, or from Congress, education, the professions, and quasi-public organizations.

There are two problems of relationship which arise with respect to the political executives. One is to gear them to the President's program. The first big step in this direction was the development of staff aides in the President's Office, particularly after 1939. The Eisenhower Administration has perfected the means by which these and the departmental political executives can work as a team. The designation of a chief of staff, the establishment of a cabinet secretariat, the revitalization of the cabinet, and the use of interdepartmental committees have helped give unity and direction to administration. The other problem is the relationship with the career officials. It is in this relationship that the combined advantages of bureaucracy and democracy are sought. Continuity, expertness, and a nonpolitical approach to problems are supplied by the career service; representation of new purpose, a broader capacity for consideration of extensive interrelationships, and a sensitiveness to popular sentiment are supplied by the temporary political officials at the apex.

Only a working partnership between professionals and politicians can supply both the knowledge and the push for the creative adaptations in policy needed in a society in flux. It is part of the function of politics to freshen and invigorate the bureaucracy and to give support to the constructive ideas which come from the bureaucracy. It is part of the merits of democracy that new ideas and new drives of a pluralistic and free society can flow through political channels to water and fertilize the bureaucracy.

Control of administration by the President requires more than personnel; it requires also an integrated structure. On the whole this has been achieved in our national administration. There are still, however, too many agencies reporting to the President, with resulting complications in co-ordination and supervision. Moreover, there are still vestigial areas of independence.

The argument for independence is based primarily on the idea that there are certain functions which should be insulated from politics. The argument is a sound one up to a point. Where activities are completely matters of expertise, as in the Bureau of Standards or in a doctor's or teacher's practice, or where law is applied to individual parties, as in payment of social security benefits or drafting of men for military service, means should be devised to prevent any political interference. The function of the political overhead is to insure that good men are selected as administrative heads, to help them get adequate resources, and to see that administration is effective. The same considerations apply where law is applied in particular cases by a judicial type of proceedings and policy evolves incidentally. But where major policy determination is the aim and primary result, then the argument for independence is anti-democratic.

Some insulation against politics in policy determination is appropriate for the protection of the public interest because politics may lead toward easy solutions. Such insulation comes in the ample presence of the permanent official with professional competence. But when the professionals have been located in administration and when process has provided for consideration of their wisdom, when in other words the politically responsible official has been informed, then the function of the professional and the justification for insulation against politics has expired, and it is time for choice in the political channel. This leaves open the question of how high the professional career service or how low the political officialdom should reach—and indeed allows this to vary from agency to agency and from time to time; it is only an argument that politics and professionalism both have a function of supply and a function of counterpoise and that the reconciliation in the public interest of democracy and bureaucracy, of politics and professionalism, comes from arrangements for each to perform its function.

What is stated is a major guide for organization and not an argument that there may not be cases where other devices for insulation against precipitate policy decisions are not justified. The guide is simply this: politics is the supreme function, but insulation against its precipitancy through a professionalized career service is not undemocratic. Representative government must assume that representatives of the people may make wrong decisions, but it need not assume that they should make them in advance of information on their effects.

The other three propositions concerning control through the representative system relate to the function of Congress. One of these is a quite obvious but significant fact: nothing is ever completely and finally delegated to administration. The Framers took care of this in solid fashion by providing for annual appropriations. Any administrator knows that where annual appropriations exist, independence expires. Also, the law-making power remains supreme, and through it changes can be made in delegations of authority and in provisions for administration. The power of investigation and inquiry is everpresent and ubiquitous. The power of confirmation of appointments completes a four-pronged battery of congressional powers, and the four prongs together beget all manner of opportunities for Congress, its committees, and its members to bring influence to bear upon administration. The influences are evoked whenever any part of administration acts in such a way as to stir dissatisfaction among any powerful groups in the nation.

Though the powers of control in the representatives of the people are adequate, their intelligent exercise is difficult for a number of reasons, all of which have become vastly more significant in one generation. One is the technical specialization in administrative functions, referred to in the last chapter. The lay mind, called upon to make judgments in a variety of fields, finds it difficult to understand the technical factors in each which must influence policy determinations. This was not so serious prior to the 1930's. Even then, in a period when new economic theories on monetary supply, compensatory spending, and the welfare state were emerging, legislators could determine many issues by practical judgment on fair play and human welfare. The new significance of defense functions and the rapid development of new methods of warfare have changed all this. Science in warfare has put a real strain on our democratic processes. Added to technicality is secrecy. Congress has always been conscious of the difficulty of breaking the curtain which administrators have often hung around the details of their work, but the secrecy engulfing scientific development and military preparations is an iron curtain for many Congressmen. Finally, there is the great complexity of public services and of the total operation of the government. Grasp of the huge military budget, of international developments on many fronts, and of such domestic problems as antitrust, industrial peace, and agricultural welfare are difficult even for the full-time executive official assisted by a staff of research and policy aides, and certainly must be baffling for the man who must spread his attention to all of these and still spend a large portion of his time with the particular problems of his constituency.

Reference to these difficulties leads to statement of our third proposition: the response of Congress to the technicality and complexity of administration and the problems with which it deals has been an extension of activity at the primary congressional working centers, the committees. Congress, like administration, senses the need for division of labor. Its ready-made and long-existing committee system serves as channel for this division. The committees are functionally-organized instruments of Congress just as the bureaus are functionally-organized units of administration. Moreover, since both the Congress and the executive will attempt to fit their functional structuralization to the responsibilities carried by government, it is natural that there should be much parallelism between the subordinate structure of the executive and that of the Congress. Congress also, like administration, senses the need for expertness. Quite accidentally this need is met in part and on occasion by the long service of ranking committee members. These members often are among the nation's most competent functional experts. V. O. Key has said that they, with the bureau chiefs, are "the cream of the career crop in the federal government."[18] But they are more likely than the bureau chief to have that synthesizing expertness, in which knowledge of technical feasibility and intuition of response of people is combined. And they may even have more of this competence than the department head who is new to government and his task. The need for expertness has been met further through the provisions of the Legislative Reorganization Act of 1946 for expert staff aides for the committees and for a high-level career group in the Legislative Reference Service.

The committees perform the functions both of counterpoise and "supply." They are points of focus through which the dissatisfactions with administrative performance can be made known to the administrative agencies, perhaps with demands for change. These demands may take the form of new legislative restrictions or they may be expressed in informal but persuasive ways. The committees are at times in open rivalry or antagonism with the administrative agencies. Norton Long has made the startling suggestion "that a loyal opposition in the upper levels of the bureaucracy could serve a function well nigh as socially useful as that performed by the loyal opposition in Parliament."[19] The committees, es-

[18] In Fritz Morstein Marx, *Elements of Public Administration* (New York, 1946), p. 346.

[19] Norton E. Long, "Public Policy and Administration: The Goals of Rationality and Responsibility," *Public Administration Review*, XIV (Autumn, 1954), 31.

pecially when the opposition party controls one of the houses of Congress, come close to performing this function of opposition criticism, even though they are outside the administrative hierarchy.

On the other hand, the committees may be working partners of the agencies. Members of committees usually develop a special interest in the types of programs with which they deal. They develop contacts with the bureaus and with the interests which support the programs administered by the bureaus. They may listen attentively therefore to suggestions for new legislation or for other support for the agencies.

The committees are so active in the areas in which they work that they become in reality co-administrators, just as the administrators are co-legislators. As Charles Hyneman has said, "Many administrative officials now receive a great deal more day-to-day guidance from Congressmen than they get from the President."[20]

The great advantage of the committee system is that it supplies additional centers of factual analysis, of initiative, and of supply and check for the bureaucracy. The great disadvantage is that it puts power to obtain concessions from administrators, to favor or punish administrative agencies, and to determine directions of policy in a small number of persons who are not representative of the nation and who are not really responsible to the houses. Expertness is obtained in Congress, but with the sacrifice of its responsibility to its parts and with the danger that these parts will not be sufficiently representative of the interest complex of the nation.

20 Hyneman, p. 159.

This points up the existence of common problems for the two branches of government. It is the reconciliation between the function of working units with specialized functions, career attitudes, and clientele connections, and the function of a more comprehensive jurisdiction, namely the presidency or the Congress as a whole, which presumably provide more adequate representation of the public interest and the public will. The ranking committee members, with tenure positions and with supporting staff services, are in a sense similar to the professional bureaucracy in the executive branch. But the Congress has left them with an independence which threatens the responsibility of the Congress as a whole, in much the same way that excessive autonomy of bureaus and commissions may threaten the responsibility of the President. And the Congress shares responsibility for the administrative problem created by the centrifugal tendencies of bureaus manned by professional personnel, for these tendencies have been accentuated by the rivalry of the committees with the President for the control of the administration.

Full solution of these problems depends upon the will of Congress to face the issue of responsibility in the same way it faced that of expertness in the Legislative Reorganization Act of 1946. This does not appear to be a possibility within the near future. But some remedy lies in a tendency already developing—namely, the service of the President to the Congress.

This leads to my fourth proposition. It is that congressional control is best achieved through the use of the presidency. The first essential for effective congressional control is the operation of control mechanisms in the office of the President. When Congress desired a tighter control over the budgets of departments, it created a Bureau of the Budget in the President's office. The Bureau has within it professionals whose professional spirit leads them to seek for excesses in the requests of departments. To the extent that they are a competent professional service, they will be the allies of all who desire to take the water out of the budget. They may not do this sufficiently to satisfy the Congress, or some elements therein, but my point is that Congress' objective is more fully attained by having budget makers in this preliminary screening position, backed by other screeners in budget offices in departments and bureaus. If, to take another example, Congress desires co-ordinated defense and diplomatic policies, its best means of attaining this is to create or authorize a mechanism in the President's office, which it has done in the creation of the National Security Council. If it desires that the proposals of policy coming to it have careful consideration of their varied effects, it should welcome the fruitful development of the clearance and program planning procedures in the Truman and Eisenhower administrations.[21]

Such central mechanisms represent the long and wide, the suprapartisan, the continuing objectives and interests of the Congress. They institutionalize a system of co-operation, which exists in substantial measure

[21] On clearance, see Richard E. Neustadt, "Presidency and Legislation: The Growth of Central Clearance," *American Political Science Review,* XLVIII (September, 1954), 641-71; on program planning, see reference at p. 131.

even though the leaders of the two branches are of opposite parties. They lift and focalize the vision of the committees of Congress to which the reports—formal or informal—of the central mechanisms are transmitted. They sift the business of government, thus saving the Congress from an even heavier load of work than it is now forced to carry. All of this is merely saying that in a hierarchical system the top board of directors cannot be efficient without co-ordinating and sifting mechanisms, and that even in our system of separation of powers the Congress will work most effectively if it regards the presidency as, to an extent, its own institutional agent.

The Congress cannot be the center of location for such mechanisms. This would weaken the power and destroy the effectiveness of the presidency, and increase the opportunities for conflict between the President and Congress. It would also weaken the supervisory and control function itself. The committees are not equipped for co-ordinative functions. They are, moreover, less representative of the nation than the President, and perhaps also less useful servants of the Congress. Only in partisan composition could they be said to be representative of the houses, for the seniority system has created a kind of "pocket borough" system for senior members and the sections of the public whose interests they reflect, and the continued affiliation of some of the committees with particular agencies, programs, and clienteles has circumscribed their perspective. Control by committees is control by segments of Congress rather than by the Congress as a whole.

Congress and the President must be coactive agents of

the public. Admittedly, the separation of powers, particularly in case of opposing party control of the presidency and one or both houses of Congress, makes their co-operation difficult. Nevertheless, institutional arrangements by which the work of Congress is geared to the presidency as an institution make it more effective in its relations with administration.

The presidency, it may be concluded, is the "centerpiece" in democratic control of the bureaucracy. It is through the President's agents working in an integrated structure that political responsibility is enforced and it is his control of the administration which creates the conditions for effective control from the Congress.

IV

I am not unmindful of the fact that the discussion in the preceding section has been limited to the problems of representative government at the national level. I plead, however, the relevance of the discussion for other levels of government. In our cities the answer to the problem of government has been sought—whether under the framework of the separation of powers in the mayor-council system or of separation of functions in the council-manager system—in concentration of administrative power in the chief executive and in gearing the work of the council to the proposals of the executive. Thus, the trends in municipalities are similar to those which have developed and which are suggested as desirable for the national government. In the states, in contrast, the governor—with some exceptions—has not been made the effective head of the executive branch

Other conditions favorable to responsible government have not developed in the states generally. Progress has been slow in the professionalization of the public service. In many states the prerequisites have not existed on either side—the operating personnel or the supervisory political structure—for a combination of the advantages of skilled bureaucracy and political responsibility, and for safeguards against the excesses both of bureaucracy and politics through a working relationship between the two. One-party factionalism or purely personal politics has been an unfavorable climate for enforcement of responsibility and hence has deterred movements for concentration of executive power.

Nevertheless, there are some states in which the model of a strong governor, a professionalized public service, and a two party system does exist. In these the most hopeful avenue for effective legislative control of administration appears to be the one running to and through the governor's office. In other states there has been some tendency toward strengthening the governor's position. Notable has been the development of the executive budget, the sometimes concentration of a group of managerial functions in the governor's office, and the enhancement of the governor's power with the development of new appointive agencies for new state unctions.

A further limitation on democratic control exists on he legislative side. The short, biennial session, with much new membership each session, is not an appropriate device for oversight of an administration dealing with numerous, diversified and technical tasks. Awareness of this fact has led to some efforts to create interim or continuing committees, to substitute annual for biennial sessions, or to make the legislative office more attractive.

The numerous variations among and within each of the states make it difficult to generalize with respect to the existence or potentialities of democratic control. Probably an increasing number will move along the lines of the national pattern whose essential features are professionalization of the public service, integration in the executive department, a continuously operating legislature, and the correlation of work of the chief executive and the legislature. Others will develop partial remedies for the weaknesses in democratic control—remedies which seem to fit the local climate, whether it be suspicion and fear of the governor, a one-party situation, a faith in amateur government, or other elements. In the long run, however, the states generally will probably move in directions similar to those at the national level.

V

We can leave this discussion of democratic control with two observations. "Nothing," said Paul Appleby, "is so representative of the public as the totality of our political processes."[22] Yet of these processes the most representative parts are those which insure attention to the total maze of interrelationships and to the ideals and needs of the body politic in its entirety. This, however, gives common purpose to the ideal of democracy and the ideal of the public interest, which is the subject of the next chapter.

22 *Morality and Administration*, p. 173.

5

The Never-Ending Search for the Public Interest

PENDLETON HERRING HAS SAID, "The *public interest* is the standard that guides the administrator in executing the law. . . . This concept," he continued, "is to the bureaucracy what the 'due process' clause is to the judiciary."[1]

There has been no history written of the concepts "public" and "public interest" in Western political thought. Such a history would undoubtedly reveal the persistence and centrality of the concepts. Cicero defined the state as a "res publica," and the Romans had a maxim that "salus populi suprema lex esto." The distinction between things public and things private formed an important part of the early history of western constitutionalism.[2] In forging the national state, European monarchs sought to identify their regimes with the welfare of the people. Modern political theorists, e.g. Rousseau and Hegel, placed emphasis on the public interest. In the United States the Supreme Court created a judicial doctrine of the public interest, President

1 E. Pendleton Herring, *Public Administration and the Public Interest* (New York and London, 1936), p. 23. Herring's italics.

2 See Charles Howard McIlwain, *Constitutionalism: Ancient and Modern* (Ithaca, N. Y., 1940).

Cleveland proclaimed the sentiment of the nation that "public office is a public trust," and politicians and writers have habitually referred to the public interest as a standard of good government.

The vitality of the concept "public interest" has not been matched by clarity in its definition. To some it is only a myth under which policy desired by the predominant will can be rationalized as that of the general interest; to others there is reality and integrity in the concept, but it is assumed rather than defined. Some, however, have sought to entrap the elusive reality in descriptive phrase.

John Dewey looked behind the term "public interest" for the meaning of the word "public." A public was created in any case where the action or nonaction of participants led to such indirect and serious effects upon others that it was "deemed necessary to have those consequences systematically cared for."[3] A public was created by the wave of *indirect effects,* and presumably the extent or intensity of the public interest would be determined by the extent of these effects. Paul Appleby took Dewey's concept and transferred the emphasis from effects of action of others to intrinsic need: "Expanding Dewey's dictum, then, we may say that a public comes into being in recognition of some need, for the meeting of which there seems—to those constituting the public—to be no satisfactory private means."[4]

Dewey's hypothesis, as he called it, and Appleby's

[3] John Dewey, *The Public and Its Problems: An Essay in Political Inquiry* (New York, 1927), pp. 15-16.

[4] Paul H. Appleby, *Morality and Administration in Democratic Government* (Baton Rouge, La., 1952), p. 21.

variation both recognize the existence of many publics. But Dewey was seeking an explanation of the state. And so he found that many publics became merged into one: "Those indirectly and seriously affected for good or for evil form a group distinctive enough to require recognition and a name. The name selected is The Public. . . . the public is a political state."[5] This comes about because officers are created to look after public interests; these officers, or the arrangements we call government, are means of representing the many needs or interests of a public nature. Dewey's concept of many publics merges, therefore, with the older concept of the public as a politically organized society.

Naturally, interests within this society do not differ in essence, though they may in complexity and diversity, from those in other groups. Within a family there are matters of conduct of individuals which are indifferent to other members of the family, other matters on which the members have conflicting interests which must be reconciled, still others where there is a deeply-shared interest. Thus, the detailed expenditure of an allowance for one member may be within an area of indifference, the setting of allowances a subject of compromise among the many family and individual needs, and the opportunity to increase the family income a shared interest. Within other groups also there are areas of indifference, areas of reconciliation, and areas of common or shared interest. This would be true, for example, of the group of cotton producers. There are many aspects of public policy to which they are, as a group, indifferent. Included within the area of con-

[5] Dewey, p. 35.

cern to them, there are deep conflicts of interest—between types of producers and between producers in different sections of the country—over production allotments, and also a common interest in the general health of the cotton economy. Similarly, within the political group there are areas of indifference—some of which are recognized by the First Amendment, areas for the compromising technique, and areas where the balancing of interests is subordinated to a dominant shared interest.

Further illustration of some of the variations in political society may be gained by a look at three approaches to the reality of the public interest. The first is through a look at those areas where there is much concentration of special interest and often much conflict among different aggregations of concentrated interest. Examples are the agricultural interest today, the conflict between shippers and railroads in the nineteenth century, and the conflict between labor and management in the twentieth. At this level of reality, a number of variations in policy making are discernible. Quite obviously, the direct interest of dominant minority or majority groups may prevail and even become the accepted view of the public interest. Herring has said that "the concept of the public interest is given substance by its identification with the interests of certain groups," and that there must be "a working relationship between the bureaucrats and special interests" which "will enable the former to carry out the purpose of the state and the latter to realize their own ends."[6] It is possible that this identification of the public interest

[6] Herring, pp. 24-25.

with group interest, and this working relationship between bureaucrats and special interests, may be carried so far that any purposes of the larger society of men will be overlooked or overstepped, and that the idea of public interest will indeed be a myth. But usually, as Herring recognized, policy making will go beyond mere identification and involve some balancing of group interests involved. Arthur Macmahon has referred to the fact that much of our legislation shows a "balancing bias" and that administrators must carry out such legislation.[7] The balancing may be only of interests immediately involved. For example, a set of legislative provisions regarding the allocation of cotton production quotas may resolve a sectional conflict among groups of producers with virtually no consideration of the impact of the compromise upon the economy, i.e., upon interests outside those of the cotton family. In such an event the public interest is involved only in the attainment of a workable compromise of immediate group interests. There will, usually, however, be indirect effects which create publics beyond the parties directly involved, and these publics then have interests which may struggle for recognition in the balancing process. In this event, the indirectly-created interests may be only additional interests to be compromised with primary or direct interests in the fulcrum of policy formation. These "public" interests may tip the scale as between the contending interests, or force compromise of all of these to some broader standard. In the latter

[7] Arthur W. Macmahon, "Specialization and the Public Interest," in *Democracy in Federal Administration,* ed. O. B. Conoway, Jr. (Graduate School, U.S. Department of Agriculture, 1956), p. 47.

case the broader standard may enable an independent public interest to become an overriding interest, at least in some degree. For example, the public interest in industrial peace in wartime led to arrangements for seizure in case of public need and subsequently the public interest in peaceful settlement was worked into a whole set of arrangements for mediation, fact finding, and temporary prevention of strikes. Beyond this, in a particular labor dispute a point may be reached where the indirectly-created public interest is vital, clear, and dominant.

A second approach to the reality of the public interest is to look for the widely and continuously shared interests which arise directly out of organic developments and shared purposes. These are interests which are so widely shared that they can be, by virtue of this fact alone, called common or public interests. Examples are the interest of people generally in education, peace, a good traffic control system, and the avoidance of boom and bust in the economy. For such cases Appleby's characterization of a public seems more adequate than Dewey's. To explain the public interest in education or a good traffic control system as indirectly-created by the action or inaction of some group or groups of persons seems less cleancut than an approach which recognizes merely that developments have occurred which create a public need. The essence of the public interest is a public need, and this need is intrinsic rather than derived. The public interest has an original, primary, and inherent quality. And it may, though confronted with or supported by claims of special interest which may obtain consideration, have a central position in policy deliberations.

There is nothing mystical about the concept of shared interests within the political society. It is no more mystical than the idea of a shared interest of family members in a larger family income, or of a shared interest of cotton producers in a healthy cotton economy. It is only broader in scope, and therefore unlikely to be shared with the same degree of universality and evenness that would exist in a compact, organic unit like the family. In practice, as a consequence, the generally-shared interest may be compromised with the interests of subgroups which do not share evenly, or perhaps at all, the prevailing common purpose. Or it may be fostered by subgroups which, in addition to sharing the common purpose, also have particular interests which will be protected or advanced by action for the common welfare.

The third approach is to look at the need for machinery for representation of interests and for weighing and deciding issues. There is a public interest in the availability of adequate organization and process, measured by the needs and ideals of society, for representing claims and resolving issues. This is to say, as Locke said, that society needs a common legislator and adjudicator, or, as we could say in more modern terms, that there is a public interest in fair and effective government, including public administration. This interest may lead to arrangements for adjudication, administration, legislation, or to supralegislative arrangements which we call constitution making. This need for public mechanism (organization and process) is the highest level of the public interest and justifies our continued concern with political "science."

The public interest, then, is diverse. It is indirectly-created interests struggling with other interests; again it is intrinsic, shared interests of all or most in substantive objectives; still again it is interest in machinery for fair consideration and for resolution of intergroup and public claims. It is no myth.

The problem, however, is how the public interest in a particular situation may be discovered. Walter Lippmann, who accepts the concept of public interest as central to "The Public Philosophy," defines it in terms of a manner of approach:

> Living adults share, we must believe, the same public interest. For them, however, the public interest is mixed with, and is often at odds with, their private and special interests. Put this way, I suggest that the public interest may be presumed to be what men would choose if they saw clearly, thought rationally, acted disinterestedly and benevolently.[8]

Since disinterested and benevolent thought arises only from a feeling of kinship and a capacity for empathy among men, Lippmann has, in brief, set up rationality and fraternity as routes to the public interest.

Some of us have sought to grasp the essence of rationality in pursuit of the public interest as involved in the process of decision. One feature of the process of decision is that it goes beyond and cuts across separate interest considerations. Appleby has declared: "But usually the interests umpired are so numerous and unlike that the process is not umpiring at all. Rather it is a process of distilling out of those private interests something approximating the general interest."[9] Mac-

[8] Walter Lippmann, *Essays in the Public Philosophy* (Boston and Toronto, 1955), p. 42.

[9] Appleby, p. 95.

mahon also sought for the kernel of rationality in decision making. Along with other perceptive comments he says, "But the essence of the public interest is *awareness of that web* ["society's seamless"] *and the constant impulse to trace things as far as possible* before acting and as a guide to action where choices otherwise unguided must be made" (my italics). Hopefully, he adds that "it is not fantastic to state this as an ideal, for it is inclination of alert and conscientious public servants."[10] I have likewise looked for the essence of rationality with respect to the public interest. It is based on full appraisal of situational factors, interests involved, and value assumptions, and hence the public interest "may be defined as the best response to a situation in terms of all the interests and of the concepts of value which are generally accepted in our society."[11] This response and the "tracing of things as far as possible"—producing broad and long vision—leads quite often to a formula or approach in policy which reveals more creative imagination and origination than umpiring, and which may be quite rational in its end result even though none of the contenders show much disinterestedness.

There are deep moral connotations in the concept of the "public interest." First, the concept is a democratic one. The word "public" is an inclusive term and its inclusiveness in the practice of government has expanded with the universality and equality of citizenship. The public is not a class or a group within society; it is all. The term gets a deeper moral meaning as slav-

10 Macmahon, p. 49.

11 Emmette S. Redford, "The Protection of the Public Interest with Special Reference to Administrative Regulation," *American Political Science Review,* XLVIII (December, 1954), 1103-13.

ery, class distinctions, and race discriminations disappear and each man becomes a first-class member of an all-embracing public. Second, the public or general interest has a certain claim to supremacy. This does not mean that claims of equity in differential justice to men shall not be recognized. A democrat and a devotee of the public interest can agree with John of Salisbury that the "prince," that is, the government, may not "have any will of his own apart from that which the law or equity enjoins, *or* the calculation of the common interest requires."[12] He may, however, be of the opinion that there is equity itself in the claims of the common interest and that it is frequently—even generally with appropriate compromises—the highest equity because it is equity for men generally.

Democracy and the public interest are related majestic concepts in our politics: both assume equality in citizenship, though both may combine this with recognition of differential justice. And the requisite of each is the consideration of all men's claims, or to put it differently, and returning to Lippmann's definition, a certain disinterestedness and other-regardedness arising from a spirit of fraternity for all.

Ideas of the public interest will differ among people, even for reasons apart from their special interests. Hobbes and Locke could differ over whether peace or rights was the first imperative of the public interest, but

[12] John Dickinson, *The Statesman's Book of John of Salisbury* (New York, 1927), p. 7. (My italics.) John of Salisbury said, "may not lawfully have any will" etc., but "lawfully" was only another word for "the intention of equity."

the difference does not prove that a public interest did not exist. Ideas of the public interest will reflect other value judgments and the organic developments in society. At one time the public interest is found in a common adjudicator to referee among property claims. At another time it is asserted, as in American constitutional law from the Charles River Bridge case in 1837 on, as a general interest which can prevail over conflicting private interests. At still another time it is viewed as planning for general economic security and for individual opportunity and security. At one time, it is identified in many states with national vitality and expansion; at a later time, it is identified with avoidance of international conflict. Its substantive content derives, therefore, from the culture of society.

The concept of the public interest is too comprehensive, too rich in variety and depth, and too penetrating in our complex life to be either escaped or canalized in a definition. It is, as Justice Frankfurter said, "A texture of multiple strands."[13] It signifies rationality and fraternity but it comprises also the balancing of claims, a certain priority for generally-shared needs and interests, an effort "to trace things as far as possible before acting," a continuing machinery for decision upon claims of interest, and response to the organic and ideological developments in society. Though this summary may leave the concept vague, it is nevertheless not an ideal laid up in heaven but a goal now for administration and government generally.

13 Federal Power Commission v. Hope Natural Gas Co., 320 U.S. 591, 627 (1944).

II

The realization of public interests in policies of government is challenged by man's egoism and society's pluralism. Our Founding Fathers were cognizant of man's basic selfishness and designed a frame of government to check its excesses. Some of them were also conscious of the essential pluralism even of the society of that day. Madison, in addition to seeing geographical alignments of interests and the class conflict between rich and poor, saw the functional divisions within the economy: "A landed interest, a manufacturing interest, a mercantile interest, a moneyed interest, and many lesser interests. . . ."[14]

But the Founders could not have foreseen the organization of functional interests which has developed. Each functional group which becomes self-conscious organizes. The organization is lighthouse and beacon to its members to inform and warn about government; it is shield and spear in their battle to escape injury or win victories through governments. Together the organizations provide a new system of functional representation which exists alongside the sectional representation provided through geographical electoral districts.

These organizations find multiple means of access to government. They lobby before legislatures and administrations. They obtain representation within the government by membership on advisory committees, establishment of agencies to serve their interests—called clientele agencies, location of professional and supervisory personnel in agencies, and by finding legislators

[14] *The Federalist,* No. 10.

who serve as their virtual agents. They support these activities by cultivation of friendships, campaign contributions, and vast publicity programs. They work at whatever center in government seems most receptive or shift from one established power center to another in the three departments of governments to find a weak point in the armor which resists them.

These associations may make our government more representative, increase the knowledge available to policy makers, and provide opportunities to the administrator to win through them acceptance for public programs. But they may also destroy the independence and the vigor of public organization.

Protection against loss of efficacy and of integrity in administration due to these activities cannot be found in administration alone. The protections must be found in society, in administration, and in the operation of the government as a whole.[15] Two questions are presented: Can we prevent the strong special interests from twisting policy for their benefit in ways which are detrimental to the public interest? Can we get a broad and inclusive, a large rather than a narrow view of the public interest? Though no complete answers can be given to these questions, it is possible to refer to a number of factors which cumulatively may give a considerable measure of protection. I shall discuss seven of these, two of which are features of our society and five of which relate to the structure and operation of government itself.

15 Those existing in administration alone are discussed in my *Administration of National Economic Control* (New York, 1952), Chapter 9.

First, there are safeguards in the nature of the pluralism of our society. The pluralism creates a social check and balance system which envelops, supplements, and gives reality to that within the government.

There are a multitude of associations, varying in size and cohesiveness. It is relevant, therefore, to consider Rousseau's answer to the problem of group interest. He feared that the partial interests of groups would destroy the general will to promote the common good. He said, therefore, "that there should be no partial society within the state."[16] This, as Madison saw, is an impossible answer for a free society. But Rousseau had another answer: "If there are partial societies, it is best to have as many as possible and to prevent them from being unequal."[17] The "desirable object would be," as Mill stated it, "that no class, and no combination of classes likely to combine, should be able to exercise a preponderant influence in the government."[18] Though interest organizations in this country are unequal in power and influence, though many of them have worked their way into centers of government, and though dominance of government at local, state, or national levels may appear to be threatened at times by some of them, we must place part of the hope for a public-interest oriented government on the check and countercheck of these organizations upon each other, and upon the ability of government because of their multiplicity to check their particularistic inroads upon it.

16 *Social Contract* (Everyman's ed., New York, 1913), Chapter III.

17 *Ibid.*

18 John Stuart Mill, *Representative Government* (Everyman's ed. of *Utilitarianism, Liberty, and Representative Government,* New York 1910), p. 255.

Further safeguard is found in the fact that most people do not give their complete allegiance to any single association. The officers of associations may claim that they speak for all the members, but usually this is an extreme claim and the officials of government know it. An individual may be a member of a family, a church, a party, philanthropic organizations, and professional, trade, or labor groups; and even though there may be a certain similarity of point of view in most of the associations to which he belongs, he may still find there is considerable variation in the policies advanced or favored by them. His attachment to his primary economic group may be qualified by his other associations. Thus, what David Truman has called multiple or overlapping memberships contribute to the safeguards of the pluralistic society.[19]

The safeguards of pluralism could become less effective. If power should be too greatly concentrated in a few large private organizations, or the primary economic associations of men should come to have a more inclusive call on their loyalties, or if the multiple memberships of particular persons all should tend to be class memberships, then the safeguards for the public interest in the composition of society would have diminished effectiveness. But industrialization creates numerous trades and professional specialties. It creates leisure and interests beyond the economic. Its tendency apparently is to divide and redivide and to create multiple interests. If our economy remains expansive and public policy is directed toward maintenance of a fluid society,

[19] David B. Truman, *The Governmental Process: Political Interests and Public Opinion* (New York, 1951), pp. 508-16.

then the protections against dominance of society by particular interests may retain their vitality.

Second, beyond the diversities of the pluralistic society are the unities which arise from the common life and the common traditions and aspirations. These unities constitute the elements of monism within society. They may be viewed in two ways—as common needs or as attitudes of mind. There are factors of common need arising from the organic developments and common aspirations of men. By way of illustration, we refer to avoidance of boom and bust, opportunity for each to employ his energies in gainful endeavor, and a measure of security for all. To an extent the administrator and the politician may appeal to these our common interests and thus moderate the demands of special groups which run counter to them. The recognition of the first named of these common interests is plain common sense; the recognition of common interests like the last two is a result of the widespread acceptance of democratic ideals. But there are other ideals of our society which may limit and circumscribe at a given moment the effect of group pressure. A few examples are the idea of fair play, the concept of reasonableness, and the idea of the rule of law. When group action and group demands seem to be excessive in terms of such ideals, the shifting middle opinion in society may rally in opposition. Even more, the statesmen in legislative, executive, and judicial posts may find opportunities to erect positive standards of future conduct which conform to these common ideals (and to common interests which they represent, though perhaps remotely) and to which groups in society must make some kind of adjustment.

David Truman has given us a valuable analysis of the importance of shared attitudes. He calls them "rules of the game" but notes that they have been referred to as "habit background" by Arthur F. Bentley, "systems of belief" by Clyde Kluckhohn, and "general ideological consensus" by Gabriel Almond. These are "widely shared but unorganized interests." They are "potential groups" which can be aroused by what Bentley referred to, without aspersion, as "demagogic leadership."[20] Popular leadership may arouse the unorganized interests, and the chief virtues of the polling place are, in my opinion, that it is—negatively—an everpresent and inescapable check on too close identification of leaders with cultivating groups, and—positively—a propulsion of leaders toward measures of public policy conforming to the needs and ideals of the society at large.

Truman reaches this significant conclusion:

> In a vigorous political system, however, these unorganized interests are dominant with sufficient frequency in the behavior of enough important segments of the society so that, despite ambiguity and other restrictions, both the activity and the methods of organized interest groups are kept within broad limits.[21]

How "vigorous" is our political system with respect to holding interest groups within limits? And how "vigorous" is it with respect to representation of the larger unities of interest? By this restatement of the major questions posited earlier we are led to the political answers for a free society containing a medley of particularistic and widely-shared interests.

20 Truman, particularly pp. 159, 348-49, 448, 511-16.
21 *Ibid.,* p. 515.

The traditional governmental answer was to provide a parallel within government to the social pluralism and check and balance system which we have listed as the first safeguard in society. The answer was pluralistic government or, differently stated, pluralistic representation and checks and balances. First through the European system of representation of estates, then through the American arrangements for representation of people and property and of people and states, and finally through the supplementation of official representation by parties and "lobbies," access to government was to be provided to each and all of the major groups. The access of each group was complemented by that of other groups. The parallel principle was checks and balances whose effect was to insure that a gauntlet of power centers would be run before any major change in policy could be effected. Together the two features—the latter one of government's internal mechanics, the former a response of government to society's structure—would presumably insure that all interests were reflected and that none could win too easily.

The effect of these features is to lead toward government by "concurrent majorities," as Calhoun called it. Decision is possible only when there is concurrence of the various interest groups which have strong access through the system of representation (official or unofficial).

The system, apart from peculiar mechanical manifestations, is being glorified today from many sources. It has its advantages for it is a kind of response to the pluralism of society. It satisfies the need of society for peaceful presentation of strong claims of interest. It is embodied fruitfully in administration through provisions for procedural due process and through the many means discussed in the last chapter for making administration responsive and responsible. But the system does not by itself provide an adequate answer to our major questions. First, the system of concurrent majorities may be one of "minority veto." It would have been in Calhoun's day, and it may be today through overrepresentation of certain minorities, "pocket borough" committee chairmanships, filibustering, interest representation in administration, and other ways. There is danger that the system of access will be overrigidified or be undemocratic, and thus deter or distort the search for the general interest. Second, there is danger, as Lindsay Rogers long ago pointed out, that the tug of rival interests can lead to stalemate when action is needed—a situation similar to that referred to in the debate of the medieval scholars as to whether an ass equally hungry and equally thirsty would die of hunger and thirst if placed equally distant from a bucket of oats and a bucket of water.[22] But the most significant limitation on the traditional answer of pluralistic representation and checks and balances is that they do not insure the overview—the broad and inclusive view of all relationships—which is urgently needed.

These deficiencies of pluralistic government point up the need for more positive approaches to supplement those of traditional theory. Are there ways by which the common interests and ideals of men can be represented in government? Are there ways in which an inclusive

22 Lindsay Rogers, *Crisis Government* (New York, 1934), pp. 62-63.

view of all relationships and of all interests—general and special—may be obtained in the practice of government? Only by answer to these questions can an adequate response be made to the problem of government.

The first of these positive methods is the second governmental answer to the questions which have been presented. It is comprehensive jurisdiction, properly balanced, of course, by decentralizing techniques. By this it is meant that for every type of problem there should be a jurisdiction which is inclusive enough to insure that all the interests involved will have a chance to be fairly considered. This is offered as a rule applicable generally to social situations. It may be illustrated by an example which will be quite familiar. Suppose it were proposed that all candidates for any degree in a university should take a political science course in public administration. Obviously the political science department, or the physics department, or the business school should not determine this issue. The decision would be one for the authorities representing the total educational enterprise of the university.

Comprehensive jurisdiction is of two types, called centralization and integration. The first is a principle of relationship among geographical units such as the nation and the states, the second of relationships among units in an organization without respect to geographical locations such as the President, departments and bureaus. The first was one of Madison's answers to the problem of divided interests. Madison, it will be recalled, was arguing in Federalist Paper Number 10 for the adoption of the Constitution, which was to set up a strong national government. Madison, who had witnessed the control of state legislatures by agrarian and debtor interests and whose philosophy of government was built upon the idea of preventing one set of interests from dominating government to the injury of others, argued as follows: "Extend the sphere [i.e. have a national government], and you take in a greater variety of parties and interests; you make it less probable that a majority of the whole will have a common motive to invade the rights of other citizens; or if such common motive exists, it will be more difficult for all who feel it to discover their own strength, and to act in unison with each other."[23]

Madison was concerned about majority domination of small government rather than minority control. He could not foresee at the moment the development of large aggregations of private, minority influence stretching across state lines. But this development confirms rather than weakens his argument. Small governments lose their capacity for fair consideration of all the interests affected when subjected to the pressure of national aggregations of influence having strength within their areas. Nor could Madison have foreseen the economic and social developments which have interwoven the parts of the nation or the world developments which have bound us in a common interest in defense. These things further confirm his argument for a jurisdiction more comprehensive than the states. Madison's nationalism (at this time in his life) is supported by the trend of history: comprehensive jurisdiction in geographical terms has been a means of protecting and promoting the

[23] *The Federalist,* No. 10.

public interest. The great issue of the future is how the need for comprehensive jurisdiction can be worked out at the international level so as to provide the protection for the universal interest in avoidance of nuclear warfare.

The other half of the answer of comprehensive jurisdiction is integration. This assumes an organization in which every problem can rise to a level where all the interacting factors affecting its solution can receive consideration. If, for example, it is a defense problem affecting army, navy, and air forces it can go to the Department of Defense, and if it is a defense problem which substantially affects general security policies and the responsibilities of the Department of State or other departments it can go to the National Security Council and the President. The argument for integration assumes that the responsibility of all units points upward to the President.

To many this is merely an argument for co-ordination. Or it is an argument for democratic control since the presidency is the only representative organ which can supply continuous and unified direction and control of administration. Here integration is argued as a route to the public interest. The argument is based on recognition that many bureaus, commissions, and even departments are clientele-oriented, and that this clientele orientation is often reinforced by associations with friendly elements in the Congress. It is based on recognition that the perspective of organizations is set, and therefore limited, by the functional allocations to them. It is based on the fact that the President is the only official of the government who is forced by direct responsibility to the one great public constituency to try to keep his mind on the public interest.

The third governmental answer is comprehensive representation. By this is meant representation of the people as a whole or, differently stated, representation of all the interests of all people through one channel. It contrasts with representation of separate groups or divisions of society, whether on the basis of class, function, or section. Sectional or geographical representation may, however, approach comprehensive representation through the single-member constituency. The Congressman representing such a constituency may find that there are many diverse interests within his district, that no one of these has a majority, that there is much overlapping of memberships and many unorganized voters. As a result he becomes a moderator among group demands and searches for answers for public problems which have a broad appeal. True, the Congressman is sometimes a virtual captive of a particular functional interest, or sometimes strongly affected by class demands, and ofttimes is representative of a sectional viewpoint. But it remains true, nevertheless, that there are many districts which are almost as pluralistic as the nation and that the single-member constituency is more favorable to search by the individual representative for the public interest than any other form of representation could be.

The chief organ of comprehensive representation is the presidency. To an extent the two-party system provides comprehensive representation, but since the national party organizations are so weak and the parties are so divided in the Congress and the nation, and the majority party is so largely under the leadership of the President, the presidency becomes the center through which the nation as a whole is represented. This function of the presidency is safeguarded to the nation through the requirement of a majority electoral vote for election of its incumbent. To win a majority the candidate must bridge the interest conflict and make his appeal on the basis of generally-shared attitudes. The function is further enforced by the high responsibility of the office. Inevitably a responsible man must try to exercise its functions for the welfare of the nation. Inevitably he will be forced to try to take a broadly-gauged view of what constitutes the general welfare. The presidency is, therefore, our most democratic and our most publicly-oriented office. And its strength and its service derive from the breadth of the constituency which it represents.

The fourth answer is creative intelligence. A careful student of American government has concluded "that the development of public policy and of the methods of its administration owed less in the long run to the processes of conflict among political parties and social or economic pressure groups than to the more objective processes of research and discussion among professional groups."[24] This is a high claim for the influence of intelligence in government. But leaving aside issues of "more or less" among factors of influence, we can agree that the creative intelligence of professional groups and of others has been an important factor in policy formation. Illustrations of the fact are numerous and should

24 Don K. Price, *Government and Science: Their Dynamic Relation in American Democracy* (New York, 1954), p. v.

deter us from seeking an explanation of the processes of government solely on the basis of pressure politics. Look, for example, at the perfection of the framework of the Public Utility Holding Company Act, and particularly at that new kernel of policy embodied in the words "single integrated public-utility system," which came from the expert consultants serving the House Committee on Interstate Commerce. Here was imagination rising from above the mountains of data accumulated by the Federal Trade Commission. Or look at the magnificent development of the Truman Policy and the Marshall Plan in those critical days when communism threatened to engulf Europe—a story told in part in Joseph Jones' recently published volume on *The Fifteen Weeks.*[25] Or look at the great imagination of those men—hardly professionals, but with first-rate educations and tremendous mental resources—who developed so quickly the techniques of allocation of scarce resources and stabilization from 1941 to 1943. Or look at the story recently told by Richard E. Neustadt of all the creative analysis that goes into the production of the President's legislative program.[26] Or look at the achievements of traffic engineers in devising means for reconciling the public interests in facilities for through traffic and local traffic, as for example in combination of high-speed, controlled-access freeways and parallel low-speed, outside lanes. The first of these examples is from the work of Congress, the next three from the work of the

25 Joseph M. Jones, *The Fifteen Weeks (February 21-June 5, 1947)* (New York, 1955).

26 Richard E. Neustadt, "Presidency and Legislation: Planning the President's Program," *American Political Science Review,* XLIX (December, 1955), 980-1021.

national executive including its administrative branches, and the last from national-state-local planning. Yet all these and others which could be recalled give hope for a large measure of that rationality which Lippmann exalted.

The opportunities for creative intelligence arise out of the complexity of the fact situations with which policy must deal. The situational factors which must be grasped are a great "complex of technologies, institutional framework, and behavior patterns."[27] All of the many ingredients of social and economic fact, interests, and ideals must be assimilated and a feasible and workable solution discovered. This hypothesis is offered: that the increase in the technicality and complexity of the situational factors which must be considered in policy making increases the need for and in the long run increases the opportunity for creative intelligence to play a part in the discovery and choice of solutions.

It is a hopeful sign that governments are awakening to the need for "braineries" at all important policy determining centers. It was this awakening which led Congress to provide for staff aid for itself in the Legislative Reorganization Act of 1946 and which led those participating in discussions on the Employment Act of the same year to seek to provide an "economic brain" for the President. It is this awakening which has accounted for the recommendation of staff aid for the President in all reorganization studies of the past twenty years, and which accounted for recommendation of aides for department heads by the task forces serving

27 Redford, *Administration of National Economic Control,* p. 230.

the First and Second Hoover Commissions.[28] It was this awakening which led my own State of Texas in 1949 to create two new staff groups for the Legislature—one to study the budget and the other to make studies of problems of legislation. The motivation was in part a desire to prevent further centralization in Washington by study of problems at the state level, but the soundest reason for public "braineries" in the states is to counteract the dependence of legislatures on interest groups for information and advice.

It is a hopeful sign also that there is recognition of the need for placing intelligence centers at the top levels of government hierarchies. When these centers are located for service to chief executives and department heads and to the legislative body as a whole there can be hope that the scope of and perspective in analysis will be as inclusive as the problems and the relationships affected by them.

The final answer on the questions we have presented is broad-gauged political leadership, adverted to earlier in this discussion of protections for the public interest. There are, of course, many types of political leaders. Some, undoubtedly all to some extent, follow the political weather vanes. Others, perhaps all to an extent, are sectional or group leaders. Some are petty, narrow, prejudiced—ill-suited for pursuit of rationality or fraternity. But some have the quality of statesmanship, at least on many types of measures. This is the apex of the synthesizing expertness we discussed in an earlier chap-

28 *Departmental Management* (Washington, 1949); *Personnel and Civil Service* (Washington, 1955).

ter. It is a kind of expertness which on the one hand draws from the knowledge which experts can give on what is possible and what is best and on the other hand senses the dominant demands of the people of the nation and merges the two in a compounded wisdom which may be more profound and more beneficent than that found either in the advice of the experts or the demands of the interest groups. This is the highest form of creative intelligence. There are men in high administrative posts who possess this lofty synthesizing competence—some of them new entrants into government service, others long-time members of the upper ranks of the civil service. These are our administrative statesmen. But this competence is more likely to be found in pre-eminent degree in some of our political leaders. These then are our ultimate safeguards for rationality and fraternity.

Our political system lifts politicians to this kind of competence in various ways. Some by virtue of the part of the country they represent or the diversified nature of their constituencies acquire a kind of "border state" psychology, that is, they do not react favorably to extreme sectional, group, or class demands but intuitively sense both the full scope of the nation's pluralism and the cross-sections of unity or potential compromise among its parts. The President, more than all other of our politicians, is forced toward this kind of psychology. In addition, some men though representing areas with strong sectional allegiances acquire, by virtue of the lack of a strong opposition party or of their strong personal positions, a kind of a career position in the House or Senate. Some of them become distinguished experts in areas of legislation and also rise to positions of leadership in the houses. They may be able to exert considerable influence toward a rational public policy in some areas, even though they may remain captives of sectional or group interests on other issues. Finally, conscience, the "impulse to trace things as far as possible," and the necessity of reaching agreement with other men may lead representatives to search for the public interest.

The emphasis on the function of creative intelligence at the administrative and political levels is not, in my opinion, anti-democratic. It is assumed, of course, that there is a large measure of public consensus, above the individual wills on particular issues, in favor of a government which operates for the common good. Moreover, the administrative expert operates under political controls and hence must infuse rather than dictate intelligence. The same is true of the politicians as a group, who are subject to compulsions and restraints from the electoral process. The danger to democracy at this stage in our development lies less in independence of will than in its subservience to partial groupings. The juncture of creative intelligence and the various forms of political responsibility which exist is essential for joint satisfaction of society's yearning for responsible government and for that rationality and fraternity which underlie the public interest.

III

Four conclusions may be stated as a result of the preceding discussion.

First, we may expect to find constant group effort to

bend public policy toward special interests. This leads to protection or promotion of special interests and ofttimes to the injury of other particular interests or to the neglect of general interests.

Second, as a result of the limitations on the power of groups in the structure of society and in pluralistic representation and internal checks, and of the existence of unities of interest and ideal, comprehensive jurisdiction, comprehensive representation, expert analysis, and political and administrative statesmanship, we may expect to find a considerable measure of public interest focus in major public decisions.

Third, we cannot expect a full measure of consistency in public policy. In a dynamic, free, pluralistic society the balance of forces which play upon government and which interact within it is constantly shifting. Within government, moves made contemporaneously at different points may not be synchronized—may even have conflicting effects—and moves made over a period of time may reflect great changes in purposes and effects. The processes of administrative and political decision are sensitive in too many directions for men to hope or to fear for the congruency of policies anticipated in the vision of a planned society. The realized public interest in a free society is no neat package of consistent elements.

Yet rationality and order will be achieved in area after area of public affairs. What is confusion today is reduced to order tomorrow. The tempests of conflicts in interest are supplanted or reduced by law, organization and process. Policies are defined in general and then crystallized in detail; system is elaborated; structure and procedure in smoothly-operating organizations reduce yesterday's problems to routine or simple management and fashion competence for tomorrow's solutions. Man moves on to new plateaus of confusion and problem. He may hope—and this is my final point—that much rationality and fraternity are embodied in the order and regularity already achieved, and that creative intelligence and broad sympathies working through institutional organization and process will yield a satisfactory measure of public good tomorrow.

6

Institutionalization of Ideal

ORGANIZATION AND PROCESS are viewed comprehensively in this epilogue as tools of community ideal. Formal organization and process are planned elements in administrative operations. Through this planning function opportunity is provided to give strength and continuity to the more persistent community needs and ideals. Included in these are the large and pervasive ideals discussed in the preceding chapters.

Organization has been the center and pivot in the study of administration. It is, as is well understood, structure and planned relationships among structural units, and is contrasted with the dynamics of behavior, the informal or unplanned elements in conduct, or the communication of ideas within organization. In theoretical discussion its prime purpose is conceived to be co-ordination. It is means of uniting or combining the efforts of men toward the effective pursuit of goal. This is, of course, only an instrumental objective; yet organization is seldom discussed in terms of its relation to ultimate objectives, such as democracy, and the public interest.

Process has received less attention than structure.

Perhaps this is because it seems less basic; perhaps also because it is more varied, for process encompasses internal procedures and public relations. In government it includes legalized processes and the less formalized procedures in policy formation and application, as well as administrative methods, now conveniently referred to in the "M" of the O and M phrase. Perhaps also the objectives in process are more diverse than in structure. Its objective may be efficient methods, or obtaining information and counsel for decision, or sustaining public consensus.

Some would regard planned process as part of formal organization. This is a loose and broad use of a term which has more clarity if limited to structure. Also, it carries danger of underemphasis of the part played by process. The O and M phrase aptly shows the insufficiency of emphasis on organization alone in formal planning. But the "M" has come to refer to production planning and managerial practice and thus has a less comprehensive meaning than process. We apparently need in our study a new term—"O and P"—to encompass adequately the institutional features of administration.

The formal elements in administration—organization and process—create shells of partial confinement for the activity of men. They also are channels of impulse for interests and ideals. They institutionalize the dominant propulsions within the community. They are a means of regularizing or—choosing another word—constitutionalizing administrative operations.

Constitutionalization, or institutionalization of ideal, is the supreme task of political science. It is the challenge to which men are ultimately led, if they are not mental eunuchs, by the work of the diagnostician and the reach for the good life. It is the task which the Framers of the Constitution and the men of Dumbarton Oaks so resolutely accepted. It is refusal, as Hamilton said, to "acquiesce in the political heresy of the poet" whose couplet read, "For forms of government let fools contest; whatever is best administered is best."[1]

Rarely do men have opportunities to build in dimensions as vast as Hamilton and his colleagues. But within the outlines of the great plan of the Framers other men have had freedom to create administrative machines and to remodel old machines which were too firmly set to send to the junk heap. Rarely, also, do they have data which will conclusively substantiate the directions of change they desire to further. They may only have enough to guide them toward an "informed" and semi-objective judgment. But this is enough—and all men should look for—in decisions in human relations, where needs, hopes, and fears of man are intermingled, and resolution of complexities outreaches the methods and myopic purposes of exact science.

II

With vast scope for ingenuity and with judgment informed as best it could be, men of the past two generations have pieced together arrangements for administration which, when combined with the surrounding political structure, institutionalize, in considerable measure, the community ideals I have discussed in the preceding chapters.

The most obvious crystallizations have been organ-

1 *The Federalist,* No. 68.

ization and process for the efficiency goal. The clearest illustration is budget organization and process. Beginning in 1921 with the establishment of the Bureau of the Budget and departmental budget offices, the budget organization has been extended downward to bureaus and other offices, and the budget process has become one of continuous sifting and screening from primary operating centers upward to Congress. Besides this there are personnel offices, O and M groups, accounting control and purchasing centers, improved organizational structures, and a convention of repeated surveys by "High Commission." These parallel developments have undoubtedly yielded a more satisfactory input-output ratio—or means-end relationship—than would have existed without them. The quest for efficiency has achieved gains through organizations and processes in which thousands of men have been and are now daily engaged. On the management side and toward the goal of efficiency, political science engineering, aided by parallels in industrial management, has been prolific in the creation of mechanism for achievement of purpose.

How are other values served by organization and process?

Organization may be viewed first as units serving different purposes. It is servant for established program aims. It is functional structures to meet those needs which have gained acceptance. It is going concerns carrying some purposes into fruition with some degree of effectiveness. Cumulatively, the sum total of organizations within administration comprise the response of society to the need for functionally-organized means for achieving particular aims. It is institutionalization of objectives which have attained success in the political process.

But organization does more than facilitate a pluralism of objectives. It is hierarchical arrangement. Hierarchy, in turn, does more than insure adherence of units of organization to separate purposes defined for them, and correlation of units engaged in related activities. It is means of insuring attention to the broader goals of society for its government.

The devices of functional allocation and hierarchy contribute to the reign of law. The organizational units are, of course, subordinate structures, confined and directed by a network of rules on finance, personnel, procedure, and other auxiliary matters, and also by the terms of their creation and of their authorizations to pursue designated purposes. But they are also structures through which society has met the need for new law. As public purposes have expanded in a complex and rapidly changing society, multiple jurisdictions have worked to establish new systems of legal order, as for labor, stock exchanges, aeronautics, and other fields, and they have usually been able to do this with reasonable promptness and with tailoring of legal rule to organic factors. Moreover, hierarchy has been a means by which large numbers of men could work at the same task under subjection to rules common to the whole undertaking. These new organizations have, I submit, been more perfect channels for uniform application of law than the traditional judicial system, with its loose administrative structure composed of weakly co-ordinated courts, juries, and attorneys. Codes, manuals, instructions, and supervisory techniques create internal cohesion and consistency in external application. And the new rule, policy guide, or decision is authoritative through the whole structure which applies policy to members of the public.

Yet all is not reducible to rule and rule itself must be made by men with discretion. Here, however, process has been supplement to organization. Administrative due process has three elements. First is the administrative search for facts. Second, by all of its many devices it may approach realization of Ordway Tead's "*principle of the representation of interests,* which says that every group which has a clearly identifiable set of interests is safeguarded in its dealings with other groups only as it has the opportunity for an explicit voicing of its interests in councils where the common problems of the several groups are under consideration."[2] Third, "decision or action is the result of the complementary contributions of units [or persons] with different competences."[3] This is departmental or institutional decision through which the span of attention and the competency for judgment by human minds may be enlarged.

Due process of the judicial type is widely used within administration, but this must be largely interstitial; the greater contribution to the facilities available to society is in the many-featured and adjustable administrative processes for fact gathering, eliciting of outside views, and collaboration within the responsible organization.

2 Ordway Tead, *New Adventures in Democracy: Practical Applications of the Democratic Idea* (New York, 1939), p. 5.

3 Emmette S. Redford, *Administration of National Economic Control* (New York, 1952), p. 28.

The ideal of administrative due process with its three components—facts, consideration of interests, and expert judgment—will be only imperfectly realized. This is ideal which can be supported only by the total operation of political and administrative institutions. Yet the goal is sought through numerous, complementary institutional methods.

It is supported in part by the institutionalization of the ideal of a competent and responsible public service. In the accumulation of rules, organization and procedure, the battle lines against the spoilsmen and for attainment of competence and loyalty to high professional standards have steadily moved forward. There is much yet to be achieved before goal can be said to have been adequately realized, but tremendous gains have been made.

The major problem is in further development of competence in general administration—of that synthesizing expertness which is able to envision interrelationships, to integrate the specialties, and to correlate technical feasibility with community purpose. Immediately, this seems to call in our national government for movement along three interrelated lines of institutionalization. The first is further development of policy aides at the departmental level. The same attention needs to be given to the development of intelligence centers on policy which has been given to creation of managerial aides. The second is consideration of the proposals for institutionalizing the generalist function within the permanent service, most recently advanced as a recommendation for a senior civil service. The third is the strengthening of the function of political leadership through the corps of political appointees responsible to the President. The last is a task of great difficulty, but is significant because it is related to the larger ideals of representative government and public interest.

The second component in administrative due process, namely, consideration of all the interests, has vast ramifications. It calls, as Tead's statement puts it, for consideration of identifiable group interests and "the common problems of the several groups." Expedients of process and organization are available through which the competence of administration for this function can be increased. The Administrative Procedure Act has institutionalized requirements for notice and hearing to insure opportunities for access for interested parties, both in adjudication and rule making. Beyond this, administration may through various devices of lay participation, through field offices, and through sampling of public opinion obtain information on community demand and response which will make it more responsive and better able to evaluate the interests of the community. More significant, probably, is integrated structure under which the larger problems of policy, raising wide and diverse considerations, are drawn upward in the hierarchy to points of consideration where perspective is broadest.

This upcasting of problems may extend to the political level. The permanent corps of administration, with its functional orientations and its separateness and inwardness, may be limited in its ability to consider and determine the interests and desires of the public, even in areas of activity already delegated to it. Politics is supplement to administration, and attainment of the larger ideals of administration is only possible through the combined activity of administrative and representative agents. The ultimate, inseparable goals of good government in free society are democracy and the public interest, and the attainment of these is dependent upon the totality of political and administrative arrangements.

In our national government overhead political control over administration is institutionalized in two channels which in part supplement and in part contradict each other. One is the congressional committee system through which the Congress seeks to give continuous and expert supervision to administration. The other is the presidency, which is both organ of control in its own right and agent of the Congress to sift, analyze and plan for it. The first undoubtedly has value in providing an external political check and means by which Congress can supply attention to problems which arise within administration and require further political action. It also creates many problems, among which is the accentuation of the difficulty of making the other channel of political control effective. Yet many trends—planned and unplanned—have led to the strengthening of the position of the President. The main tendency of planned efforts in the past two generations has been to supply the President with facilities for effective control of administration. This, we have argued, is institutionalization of congressional control, as well as of presidential control, for it is a means of informing the judgment and focusing the attention of Congress.

The political and administrative systems together institutionalize in a number of ways the search for the public interest. The essence of this search is the tracing of "things as far as possible" within a comprehensive frame-work. The tracing of things has been facilitated by the development of staff aides in the President's office and of means for the Congress to obtain facts to aid it in legislation. It may be facilitated by the further development of policy aides in departmental offices. The creation of thought centers at the upper levels of our government provides opportunities for creative intelligence to be applied to the solution of problems, often in advance of the crystallization of particularistic viewpoints by special interests. Comprehensive frame-work is provided on the administrative side in integration up to the President's Office. It is provided on the political side in the position of the President as the national representative, in the single-member constituency, and in those factors which raise particular members of Congress to positions of independent, responsible national leadership on certain types of issues.

There are, as any realistic observer knows, a multitude of ways and of opportunities for special interests to use government, including administration, for their benefit, even though this may not be for the general good. Yet, and this is our point of emphasis, the influence of the special interests is only part of the story; the rest of the story is that the ideal of the public interest is embodied in institutional framework in ways which give it reality in the process of government as a whole and of administration in particular.

In our cities real progress toward institutionalizing the ideals of democracy and the public interest has been made in the development of new forms of organization and in the reach for expert personnel. In the cities the trend has been toward a professionalized service, integrated administration, and correlation of the work of councils with that of chief executives. In some states the process of institutionalization has paralleled that for the nation and the cities, but considering the states as a whole the attainment of the ideals of efficiency, competent and responsible men, democratic control, and the public interest has been hampered by delays in professionalizing the public service, fear of integrated administration, one-party factionalism, and the failure to develop the legislature into an effective organ of continuing action. Nevertheless, the twentieth century has been a period of great change in state administration with considerable movement along the same lines of institutionalization as in our national and municipal governments.

III

I think the final answer to those who would charge administration with lack of "well-defined ideals" is that they have not viewed it with perspective. They have not seen organization and process as servants of a society which has demanded an expanded role for government. They have not taken the measure of the great drive for efficiency and for competence and responsibility in the public service. They have not adequately contemplated the necessity and the great boon to society in the combination of functional specialization and integration. They have not fully comprehended the subordination of administration to representative government, the many methods by which law and discretion are combined in fair and effective administration, and the means through which the public interest is partially attained.

There is, of course, a great gap between ideal and reality. Administration is manned by human beings and is the servant of a complex society. The frailties and inadequacies of men and the divisions, selfishness, and ignorance within the society are reflected in administrative operations. Yet organization and process are vehicles of rationality and common purpose. They are means by which particular objectives of policy desired by the dominant will are given continuity and force; beyond this, they are the means by which the abiding and all-encompassing values of society become ubiquitous in the practice of government. The final safeguard in administration is that the shared will within the society for efficiency, rule of law, informed judgment, competence, supremacy of representative government, and the public interest has been incorporated, and may be further incorporated, into arrangements which check and direct the actions of men, and which in significant measure provide channels for the constitutionalization of administrative practice.

Index